The Book That Has Changed Thousands of Lives!

"Leverage is the key to great wealth." - Robert Kiyosaki

LAW OF LEVERAGE

THE KEY TO EXPONENTIAL WEALTH

RANE A. PANALIGAN, CPA

Order this book online at www.trafford.com
or email orders@trafford.com

Most Trafford titles are also available at major online book retailers.

Cover designed and layout by: Raul A. Panaligan Jr.
Illustrated by: Catherine Ritch

Print information available on the last page.

ISBN: 978-1-4907-3851-2 (sc)
ISBN: 978-1-4907-3853-6 (hc)
ISBN: 978-1-4907-3852-9 (e)

Library of Congress Control Number: 2014910515

Trafford rev. 05/21/2015

 www.trafford.com

North America & international
toll-free: 1 888 232 4444 (USA & Canada)
fax: 812 355 4082

TODAY
A READER

TOMORROW
A LEADER

Freedom
Is what we have -
Christ has set us free!
Stand firm, then,
As free people
And do not
Let yourselves
Be burdened again
By a yoke of
Slavery.

- Galatian 5:1

_____

Date

This book is a gift for

_____

Name

_____

If found, please return to owner

_____

Contact No.

DEDICATION

This book is gratefully dedicated, above all, to Almighty God, who unceasingly gives me the wisdom and the guidance to share His principles of abundant life. To God be the glory;

To the millions of people who have lost their jobs, to those who are being tracked down by their creditors, to those who have unwittingly lost their savings and to the same multitude who have lost hope in attaining a prosperous living;

To every Filipino who dreams and aspires to break their bondage with personal poverty to achieve financial and time freedom so they may be of great service to others;

To every Filipino leader who wishes to become the architect and building block of our economic society for the betterment of the standard of living and towards the establishment of a strong republic;

To every individual who yearns to understand the in-depth knowledge of the principles, systems, and framework of the networkpreneurship industry;

To my beloved parents, Mr. Raul P. Panaligan Sr. and Mrs. Neriza Amarrador Panaligan, who inspires me to pursue my dreams and mission in life;

To my brother Raul, sister Mary Jane, and in-laws Liza and Michael, my business partners, best friends who gives unconditional support, and those who helped wholeheartedly in the completion of this book—this humble publication;

To my five adorable nieces, Ciara May, Lauriza Jane, Lira Joy, Lira Grace, Lara Faith and nephew Raul Martin—our family's delight;

And to West Mindoro Academy and Philippine School of Business Administration, my Alma Maters.

FOREWORD

"Give a man a fish and you feed him for a day; teach him how to fish and you feed him for a lifetime." - Lao Tzu

Each one of us has a deep, driving desire we wish to gratify. In order to bring our ambitions and desires to fulfillment, we must possess one important factor and be successful in managing it—money.

Money is symbolical of life's energy and sustenance. As a medium of exchange, we earn and utilize it to accomplish our goal. Money earned is the value of products and services we render for the convenience of others.

Success in life is the progressive realization of one's goals and the fulfillment of his/her own dharma—the highest purpose of living in the service of others.

The prosperity of a nation depends on the financial wellness of its citizens. Wealthy citizens establish a wealthy nation. Financial literacy, wealth consciousness and leverage system are the keys to achieve prosperity.

This book deals with wealth and life-building principles that will lead you to the right perspective and careful projection of your goals. Use and abide by the principles you will learn in the succeeding pages, and let them guide you towards an abundant, happy and purpose-driven life.

Like the Law of Gravity, the principles contained in this book are universal. Let these principles lead you to the realization of your goals, as it has been proven by so many, time and time again.

CONTENTS

CHAPTER IV – PRINCIPLES OF PROSPECTING

CHAPTER V – GOAL SETTING AND TIME MANAGEMENT

CHAPTER VI – CODES OF LEADERSHIP

CHAPTER VII – FOCAL POINT

Chapter I

RIALITIES
OF LIFE

📖 Life is a Choice

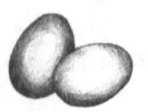

Two eggs are telling each other what they wanted to be when they hatch, with the first egg wanting to be an oyster, which just stays in the water and lets the ocean take control of its life. The first egg wants a secure existence, with no decisions to make and no responsibilities to accomplish. The second egg, on the other hand, wishes to be an eagle–even if it is responsible for hunting its own food and making survival decisions, it is free to go wherever it wants and fly as high as the highest mountains. The second egg wants to be in control– with no limits placed on him– therefore creating its own destiny.

What role would you like to portray in real life–that of an oyster or that of an eagle? The choice is yours!

"You are what your deep, driving desire is. As your desire is, so is your will. As your will is, so is your deed. As your deed is, so is your destiny." - Indian Philosopher

"Life without freedom is no life at all." - Braveheart

The Social Security Service Survey
According to the 1995 Social Security Service Statistical Population Sampling on the status of an average Filipino when they reach the age of 65:

> 45% are dependent on relatives,
> 30% are dependent on charity,
> 23% are still working, and only
> 2% are financially independent.

To which category would you like to belong when you reach the retirement age: the 45%, the 30%, the 23% or the 2%?

People do not plan to fail, they just fail to plan. Remember, the best person to take care of you when you get older is the younger person you are today. Plan ahead!

"It is a useless life that is not consecrated to a great ideal. It is like a stone wasted on the field without becoming a part of any edifice." - Jose Rizal

📖 Are You Living Just to Survive?

 Once there was a group of foxes discussing what their lunch would be for that day, and they spotted a rabbit in the greener side of the valley. One fox wasted no time and chased after the rabbit, which ran as fast as it can to elude its predator. The fox tried its best to catch up, but after several hours of running after its prey, it got exhausted and eventually gave up the chase. The rabbit, now certain that nobody's running after him, went into the direction of the forest and disappeared.

What do you think was the reason why the fox did not capture his target lunch? Obviously, the fox and the rabbit have a conflict of interest. Both run after something but from a different perspective: The fox was running only after its lunch while the rabbit is running for his life.

What about you, my friend, are you thriving only for your lunch or for your life?

According to the 2014 SWS (Social Weather Survey) third quarter ratings of typical Filipino families are 55% classified below the poverty line. These families do not only see, smell, taste, hear, and touch poverty—they actually breathe it every day. Then, how can we, as a nation, establish a strong republic if the citizenry's economic welfare is impaired? How can we survive this reality?

Poverty is indeed one of the foremost problems we have to address and find ways to resolve. I believe that individual poverty can trace its roots from a person's core values itself. To uplift the

3

economic condition of our country, we must be able to accept new ideas on how we view the world in its entirety.

Each of us should empower one another and thrive not only to live but to lead a better life. Through entrepreneurial mindset, esteemed empowerment and self-discipline, we can elevate the quality of our living and settle in a strong republic. And that change should start from each one of us.

"The significant problems we face cannot be solved at the same level of thinking we were at when we created them." - Albert Einstein

The Rat Race

 A study shows that 80-90% of average people experience Rat Race, also known as the race for survival or the 15/30 scheme. When we talk of money, we instantly think of work. Thus, to work hard for someone else's benefits in a business we do not even own. We work laboriously all our life struggling for financial stability and job security but sadly is left with so little time when we reach the retirement age.

In reality, our fears and desires impels us to do earn more. It is the fear of not having the money to spend that drives us to work harder; for fear of not settling our monthly bills and other financial obligations. It is our fear that obliges us to stay up late to earn that extra money. The moment we receive our paychecks, our fear is replaced by our desire to compensate for our needs and convenience.

Then a pattern is set: we get up early, go to work, receive our 15th-day paycheck, then pay our bills and consume for our necessities. We get up early again the next day, go to work, wait for our 30th-day paycheck and do the same things all over again.

Our life, therefore, becomes a perpetual habit of our two emotions—our fears and desires. Even though we are offered a larger sum, the cycle continues with additional spending and a corresponding tax increases. That is why it is called the rat race or the race for survival, it shows that a person does the same thing in his/her life over and over again but is not fairly compensated for his/her hard work. These people move everywhere but actually go nowhere. They are trapped in a financial dilemma; they are beating the red line finances; and their income is almost equal or lesser than their actual expenditures.

Money dilemma is not solved by ignorance but by intelligence. Free your mind and train yourself to become financially literate. Liberate your financial consciousness and you will discover a wide range of opportunities to earn more at a lesser time. The power of money is your vantage point. Be the master of your own finances and let the money work for you.

Use your fears and desires for your benefit. Let not your emotions overpower your thoughts. The choice is yours.

"If we want to change a situation, we first have to change ourselves. And to change ourselves effectively, we first have to change our perception." - Stephen Covey

Economic Trend

7T BC-1700+A.D.	*Agricultural Age*
	Those who have the land own the wealth.

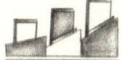

1740-2000 A.D.	*Industrial Age*
	Those who have the machinery own the wealth.

21st century

Information Age

Those who have the right ideas, information and network own the wealth.

"In the 21st century, we are not talking about the 'Have or the Have-Not' but the 'Know and the Know-Not'." - Billy Lim

"We are now being given a preview of some of the things to come... the new millennium will surely see not only changes but a rapidity of changes that will truly leave us breathless." - Mahathir Mohamad

Future Shock

Most of us has a fair knowledge of the past (history), the present (current events), and the after-life (religious aspect), but very little about the future.

The following are some of the inevitable crucial events that are transpiring right now and in the near future:

1. The world is getting smaller and smaller because of technological advancement. We are now living in a borderless world of instant communication (Internet and cyberspace), globalization and free enterprise. There would be an emergence of universal connectivity. The glue that traditionally holds together all economic activities will rapidly melt in the heat of universal connectivity and will separate the flow of information from the flow of things for the first time in the history of man. The whole world will link through one mentality—to become a global citizen transcending all beliefs, culture and race to one global community.

2. The consolidation and merging of giant companies will make competition a key adversity. Big fish versus big fish. Entrepreneurial business, Franchise, and Network Marketing are the most viable

business alternative that can survive the rapid economic changes. Those hooked up in the Internet and other satellite technologies are potential competitors. One must not underestimate or dissuade small competitors and must thrive instead for world-class. The forces of free enterprise and competition will thrust the quality up and the cost down. Customer satisfaction should always come first.

3. The movement of wealth creation from financial capital to human capital. Wealth creation has gone from money to people—both intellectual and social. There will be a massive rate of unemployment and underemployment due to dramatic shift in our economy from industrial age to knowledge worker age. A new economic system will emerge with new mind set, skill set and tool set that will drive the new global economy. The employment sector will evolve in a free-agent market and people will have more and more options to express their potentialities.

4. With the information overload, you must know how and when to eliminate useless or garbage information. We are now in the era of knowledge-based economy where right information and network are the key factors for personal growth and financial prosperity.

5. The Power Shift: If the 21th century belongs to the politicians, the 21st century is for the entrepreneurs. We are now being introduced to the age of individualism—the expression of one's economic, social, mental and spiritual freedom.

We currently live in perhaps the best time in human history where opportunities and possibilities for immense individual growth are inevitable. The explosion of new information and technology has accelerated the changes in the information age. The intense competition in almost all fields of endeavor placed the world in the golden era of radical transformation and growth.

"In the 21st century, the rule of money has changed. The rule states that: You are now your own economy— you are now 100% responsible for creating your own wealth and increasing your financial leverage in solving your money problems, in simple terms, our Financial Intelligence and Leverage determines our own economy."

- Rane A. Panaligan

"The entrepreneurial mindset continues to thrive at Microsoft because one of our major goals is to reinvent ourselves—we have to make sure that we are the ones replacing our products instead of someone else."

- Bill Gates

You are Involved!

Underdeveloped Country (small fish vs. small fish)

Poverty prevails. White-collar workers are very few and most people earn a living through small-scale enterprises.

Developing Country (big fish vs. small fish)

The nation is in progress. Large amount of capital is needed to build infrastructures, purchase updated machines and equipment and export products for global competition. The government encourages the growth of big corporations and for them to join the stock market. Bigger corporations eventually leave the small competitors on the sidelines.

Developed Country (big fish vs. big fish)

When big corporations outsell the small-scale enterprises, entrepreneurs will most likely end up as white-collar workers. These workers are more learned, more aggressive and may be difficult to handle. They may bargain for higher wages and more benefits. Company strikes may occur if terms are not met. With the increase in the number of the learned and the middle-income group will spring more company politicking groups. A corresponding increase in welfare services means collection of higher taxes.

Results:
Middle-Class Workers

Their demand for better wages and more benefits means inflation and collection of higher taxes. The country may be rich, contrary to the poor status of its citizens. The dream of buying a new house, a new car or other properties will remain a dream. A living wage is not even met by the minimum wage and cannot keep up with inflation. If the gap between the rich and the poor is in its extremity, chaos may occur and result to major socio-economic change.

Small and Medium Enterprises

These types of businesses may find it hard to keep up with the intense competition. They might not be able to adjust to the drastic and frequent changes in the market due to technological advancement. Entrepreneurial marketing, superior service and continuous innovation are the key factors in outperforming the big boys of the business.

Big Businesses

No matter how big or small a corporation is, marketing their products plays a vital role. Stiff competition and large investments are crucial for survival. Big companies merge and consolidate to flex their financial capabilities and provide a better leverage against other big business entities.

The financially powerful firms will employ more skilled workers and managers, procure highly productive equipment, import or patent the latest technology and production techniques, find more affordable but quality production materials and access more market.

They are able to convene a stronger force for combat and acquire a critical mass, which is a prerequisite for their success.

That trend is prevalent in developed countries. Through merger and consolidation, business entities can maintain a favorable market share without having a detrimental effect on their business equity.

"Massive changes are taking place at an amazing rate in every arena of life. This rapid and complex change is so dramatic that they are more accurately referred to as paradigm shifts. A Paradigm can be defined as the way we perceive the world, a shared set of assumptions or belief systems. As we face 21st century, we find ourselves in rapidly shifting paradigms, which seem very destabilizing and chaotic. At the same time, we are creating new paradigms in the form of innovative products and technologies, New Business and Industries." - Allan Walter

What's Missing with Schooling?

The word *education* comes from the Latin word *educo*, meaning to lead out or bring it out. An expression of an idea or an exchange of information brings about education; we bring out the talent and intelligence that we are borne with to guide us through life. Thus, "Non-schola sed vita discimus", as a Latin saying goes. In English, we say, "We do not learn for school but for life."

What is missing with education is its concept of literacy. We learn about professionalism and career moves to secure a job in a business owned by others, but fail to learn the value and wisdom behind wealth creation or "financial literacy" to attain security. Financial illiteracy is the root of our financial struggle. Majority of the population is professionally literate but financially illiterate. They work for money instead of making money work for them.

The economic life span, or the ability to earn of an individual, ranges from 30 to 40 years. He may be financially stable at age 25 then work and work until he or she reaches 65, then seek retirement.

Table 1.A

Pre-school.................................	3 years
K-12	12 years
College	4 years
Post College	4 years
Total average years in school.....	**23 years**

Table 1.A above shows that one-third of our life is spent in school and the remaining two-thirds is spent working for other people. Financial struggle is often the result when people work all their lives for someone else and still end up saving nothing when retirement period comes.

Dear friend, mind your own business. You have all the birthright to explore your hidden potentials and thrive for success. I am not against education, in fact, I highly advocate it. We only have to put its system in the right perspective.

"The main reason why people struggle financially is because they have spent years in school but learned nothing about money. The result is that people learn to work for money... but never learn to have money work for them." - Robert Kiyosaki

Thomas Stanley, author of the breakthrough book *The Millionaire Mind* made a close study on the success of over a thousand self-made millionaires in United States. He said, *"You need guts, not good grades, to become rich. Grades don't measure tenacity, courage or leadership. The statistics demonstrate that most millionaires did not achieve high test scores or grades or even went to top schools. What I found consistently, is that of all the factors involved in financial success, hard work was first, and graduating at the top of the class ranked last... IQ is no indicator of success. Millionaires build empire on creativity and common sense. They focus on a goal, take calculated risk, and then work harder than most people."*

Most of the financially successful individuals interviewed by Stanley practically started with nothing. Some got D's or worse back in school. Some dropped out. Others have learning disabilities and a number of them were even humiliated by their parents and teachers because they were not as smart as their classmates.

Some of them have left school without finishing their college degrees: Henry Ford, founder of Ford Motors Co.; Thomas Edison of General Electric; Ted Turner of CNN; Ralph Lauren of Polo; and Bill Gates of Microsoft.

A college education may be important for traditional professionals but not with the likes of Bill Gates and Henry Ford, who found great wealth with their special abilities and innovative ideas. They were able to establish their own business empires that made them exceedingly financially successful.

"It is a fact that if you want to attain financial freedom, you must be involved in an occupation that is going to allow you to do so. I have got nothing against working for a living, but you must understand that a job is just for surviving, and not for the creation of wealth. If you want to be wealthy, you must never make working for others a lifelong endeavor." - Eddy Chai

Even former education secretary of the Philippines Andrew Gonzales said, *"The country's dropout rate in elementary, secondary and college education is very high. Of the 100 students who entered Grade 1, only about 68 finish Grade 6. Of the 68 high school students, only about 48 graduate. Of this number, only 26 enroll for college, and only 16 earn a degree".*

He said that the above phenomenon is not necessarily bad, that many dropouts did good and even better than college graduates. They learned and graduated from UHK (university of hard knocks). Their wise and great teacher is the life experience. It is unique because it gives you first the test before it teaches you the lesson. And the lessons that you may learn from it will help you in becoming an effective and strong-willed person.

Secretary Gonzales even suggested that a non-formal education on entrepreneurship could be an alternative to a college education. As long as a person is hard-working, persistent, and is in the right direction, financial success is not difficult to achieve. So do not lose hope even if you are a dropout, you can start up!

"Formal education will make you a living. Self-education will make you a fortune." - Jim Rohn

Idea Revolution

"There is one thing stronger than the entire world and that is an idea whose time has come." - Victor Hugo

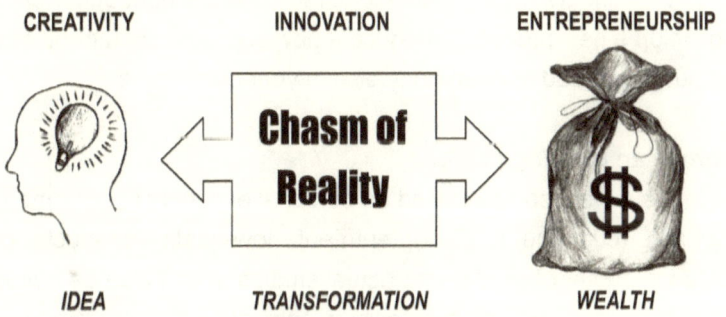

| CREATIVITY | INNOVATION | ENTREPRENEURSHIP |

Chasm of Reality

| *IDEA* | *TRANSFORMATION* | *WEALTH* |

(Adapted from Zimmerer and Scarborough)

"The single most powerful asset we all have is our mind. If it is trained well, it can create enormous wealth in what seem to be an instant." - Robert Kiyosaki

Ideation is the process of searching for a worthy and effective niche or market. Through creativity, new ideas can be introduced. It opens opportunities for possible business ventures and it is where entrepreneurship begins—the idea creation.

Be aware of everything

There is no other way to know what is happening around you but to research. Be aware of everything that can help you identify a market gap (demand or supply gap) to pursue a viable business.

Recognize a need

Determine what product or service is marketable in a particular event or situation. Talent and ingenuity is inherent to an entrepreneurial person. If you are sensitive to the growing needs of man, then you are the right person for the job. Incorporate your ideas and create your own demand/supply gap for the establishment of a new business.

Recognize trends

Entrepreneurs must be able to tell when is the right opportunity to develop a new product. Introduce a new style and set a trend that can put you ahead of everybody else in your own market.

Improve an existing product

Improvement can be based on personal experience, customers' feedback (customer's discontentment, low-quality products or existence of other brands) and actual studies. It can also be based primarily on the product's capability to compete with other products of the same kind. Improvement of a product can open its doors for innovation, which can possibly send out a new product.

Question assumptions

Challenge yourself and question the status quo. The quality of a product or a service must motivate your intellectual and innovative mind to explore the possibilities of a new concept for a new product. This will enable you to venture in another business for your new discoveries.

Name it first, and then develop it

If you were able to see, find, or learn a new concept first, grab it! It may be a venture worth nurturing. Study the possibility of developing the idea and put it in a business blueprint. Instead of turning in a good idea to someone else, develop it yourself. In the long run, a good product or service borne out of your idea will speak for itself and may mean a favorable business undertaking for you.

Combine industries

After a thorough research, adapt the most feasible idea and trend that can measure up to your field of expertise. Organize a business plan or system to meet your objectives. Be creative and think of all the possibilities.

(Adapted from Lambing and Kuehl)

"Creative thinking involves breaking out of established patterns in order to look at things in different ways."

- Edward De Bono

Ideas That are Worth a Business

Need/want driven

Money savers

Time savers

Incorporating a unique or strong competitive advantage
Linked to personal talent, ability, or specialized knowledge
Can improve one's earning
Can satisfy basic and extreme needs of man
Contribute to solving socio-economic problems
(Adapted from *Igniting Innovation* by Kari Lampikoski & Jack Emden)

"An idea well expressed is like a design of gold, set in silver." - *Proverbs*

The Paradigm

The word *paradigm* came from the Greek word *paradeigma*, which can be defined as a perception (a pattern of thought); a frame of reference; a way of viewing reality; or lens through which we see the world.

This term encompass our self-definition and awareness in relation to our existence and social ecology.

OLD PARADIGM	NEW PARADIGM
Avoid and fear change	Change is constant
It's good enough	Zero defect/Six Sigma
Management	Leadership
Monopoly	Global competition
Industrial Age	Information Age
Profit oriented	Service oriented
School/University	E-Learning
Academic excellence	Street-smart
Employment	Entrepreneurship/Networking
Salary/Fixed Income	Residual Income/MSI
	(Multiple Sources of Income)
Synthetic medicine	Natural medicine
Political empowerment	People empowerment
Laborer/Employee	Associate/Partner

Typewriter	Computer
Postal Service	E-mail
Poverty consciousness	Wealth consciousness

"Change is the law of life and those who look only to the past or present are certain to miss the future."

- John F. Kennedy

📖 The Paradigm Shift

A naval battleship is struggling against bad weather when the lookout cried that they are heading towards a steady light and is close to collision. The captain advised the other ship to change its course but the seaman answered that the battleship changed its course instead. The irritated captain insisted that the other ship change its course immediately which prompted the seaman to reply that they are heading to was actually a lighthouse. In that instant, the captain quickly maneuvered the battleship in the other direction.

Oftentimes, when faced with reality, we could not easily or readily give up our firm beliefs. We find it hard to change our views in an instant if we are not enlightened. Like the battleship's captain who stands firm in his orders but gave way when warned, we should be adaptable to change. In life, we always have a choice. Like water, we must be adaptable with unexpected circumstances.

Change is the foundation of growth. We have to change our own paradigm for the better course of our life.

"Be formless, shapeless, like water... You put water into a cup, it becomes the cup; you put water into a bottle, it becomes the bottle; you put it in a teapot, it becomes the teapot... Now water can flow, or it can crash, be water my friend." - *Bruce Lee*

5 Years Ago, Today, and 5 Years After

Come to think of it: If you keep on doing what you have always done, chances are, you will get what you have always got and maybe it is about the right time you decide what you really want to do with your life.

If your problem five years ago is of financial nature and you still have that same problem today, maybe there is something wrong with the way you handle money matters effectively. If you would not improve on your system, it is possible that you will still have the same money problem five years after.

Progress is impossible without change, and those who cannot change their minds cannot possibly change anything. If you want to rectify something, you have to know where you want to go or else, it is not going to happen. You have to decide this very moment if you want to achieve a significant change in your life.

Real change should emanate from our inner being. One who cannot change the very fabric of his thought will never be able to transform his or her dreams into realities and will not make any advancement. Real change must hit on the fundamental and essential paradigms that define our character and must create the lens to which we peek to see the world.

Be here now! Your future starts today.

"It is in your moments of decision that your destiny is shaped." - Anthony Robbins

Definition of Material Wealth

Material wealth is defined as that status of an individual's existing financial resources that supports his/her way of living for a longer duration, even if he/she does not work to generate a recurring income.

Your material wealth depends on the number of days you can survive without employing your productive labor but still maintain your basic standard of living. It is not about how much money you make that counts but how much money you have saved and how long can that money work for you that greatly matters.

If you have a ₱200,000 bank savings and a monthly expenses amounting to ₱50,000, your material wealth is approximately 4 months or 120 days only. Wealth is measured according to the period of time, not in pesos or any other monetary forms.

"Wealth does not necessarily mean having millions and millions of pesos. Being wealthy simply means having the financial resources to support your chosen lifestyle. Wealth is nothing more than having money to fund your particular needs at any given time." - Francisco Colayco

The 5 Principles of Material Wealth

I. Wealth comes gladly and in increasing quantity to any man who will put by not less than one-tenth of his earnings to create an estate for his future and that of his family.

II. Wealth works diligently and contentedly for the wise owner who finds for it profitable employment, multiplying even as the flocks of the field.

III. Wealth clings to the protection of the cautious owner who invests it under the advice of men wise in its handling.

IV. Wealth slips away from the man who invests it in businesses or purposes with which he is not familiar or which are not approved by those skilled in its keep.

V. Wealth flees the man who would force it to impossible earnings or who follow the alluring advice of tricksters and schemes or who trusts it to his own inexperience and romantic desires in investment.

"Wealth consciousness is so much more than simply having the ability to make money. It's a mindset that involves seeing life, not as a struggle, but a magical adventure where our needs are met with grace and ease. Wealth consciousness is a state of mind, a sense, not of believing, but really 'knowing' that what we need is available to us." - Deepak Chopra

The Pipeline

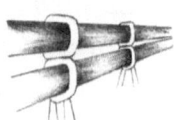 Once there was a town, whose water is very scarce, and the elders proposed a bidding of contract to have water delivered to their town on a daily basis. Two young men, Pedro Mangunahan and Juan dela Cruz, offered their services, with Pedro running back and forth from the lake every day, with two galvanized steel buckets, to fill up a large concrete holding tank the townspeople had built. Juan, on the other hand, left the town for a few months, wrote a business plan, created a corporation, employed a President for monitoring, found four investors, and later returned with a construction crew that built a large stainless steel pipeline that provides cheaper and cleaner water than Pedro's, 24 hours a day, seven days a week. Pedro tried to compete with Juan by lowering his prices and hiring his two sons for extended service hours, but no matter how hard Pedro worked, Juan's system of water delivery earned more with the millions of buckets delivered every day, creating a pipeline not only delivering water to faraway places, but a pipeline of money going directly to his own pocket.

Now, ask yourself: Am I building a pipeline of wealth or hauling buckets of poverty?

May this story guide you in your journey to financial and time freedom.

"Money is plentiful for those who understand the simple laws which govern its acquisition." - Arkad

Where is Your Cash Flow?

Employment	-	You have a job (Employee/Laborer)
Self-employed	-	You own a job (Professional/Specialist)
Business	-	You own a system (Entrepreneur)
Investment	-	Money works for you (Investor)

Robert Kiyosaki observed that every person generates his or her income in at least one of the four quadrants of the *Cash Flow Quadrant*. Traditionally, we look for a stable job after earning a college degree. We work for money or a salary, which is the least secured of all sources of income. A salary will never give you financial freedom and working for other people is like sowing seeds in other people's field.

The 'I-do-it-myself' or the self-employed belong to Quadrant 3. They are perfectionists in their own niche. These people are too attached with their work system and eventually become the systems themselves. They seldom delegate their work to others. They believe that nobody can do the job better. Money to them is secondary; recognition comes first.

The employed or employee and the self-employed or professional (Quadrant 4 and Quadrant 3) cannot entrust or delegate their work to others. Both groups practice the 'power of singleness' which, more often than not, denies their capacity to earn more by relying too much on their own selves because it is the nature of their job. Higher income means greater responsibility and hard work. The employed and the self-employed belong to the category of 'no work, no pay' individuals and are highly motivated by security.

On the contrary, those who belong to Quadrant 1 and Quadrant 2 (business and investment) respectively, have a different emotional and psychological temperament or internal core values. They are highly motivated by freedom.

In the business quadrant, the players are full pledged entrepreneurs. Their enterprise is their playground. Like a true man of business, an entrepreneur owns the system and the system works for him. Delegating his work to others is not a problem.

Three business systems goes well with this quadrant: (1) the *conventional* company or corporation, where you can develop your own system; (2) the *franchise*, where you can buy an existing system; and (3) the *alternative franchise* (network marketing), where you can buy a system and be a part of that existing system.

If any of those systems efficiently operates, it can provide a long term and stable stream of income with least physical effort on the part of the owner.

Out of the three, the Alternative Franchise is the easiest to handle and operate. This system has a minimal capital outlay and has a high-potential source of substantial residual income. Your time and effort are the crucial factors in managing this type of business organization.

The Quadrant 4 is the Investment quadrant, the playground of the rich. If you already have a steady source of residual income, you may invest your money on another business. This quadrant will give you compounded interest and compounded growth that generates from your assets. Money will work for you.

Individuals from the Quadrant 3 and Quadrant 4 are motivated by security and stability while the last two quadrants will lead you towards the path of financial freedom.

Which quadrant would you prefer?

"Wealth is the product of man's capacity to think." - *Ayn Rand*

The Mindset: Poor – Middle Class – Rich

Factors	Poor	Middle Class	Rich
Who	Employees, laborers	Employees & self-employed	Entrepreneurs and investors
Education	High school or college graduate	Values a college education	Values only "street smart" education acquired from peers/self-learning
Most valuable resources	Paycheck salary	Short term Investments	Time and long term investments
Resources focus	Salary or hourly wage	Net worth (home and personal effects)	Cash Flow, Net worth (real asset) and Network
Time setting	Next payday	Long-term	Adapt to each financial goal or investment
Major financial goal	To survive until next payday	To built up a vast net worth by age 40 to 65 years old	Financial and time freedom
Cash Flow Management (CFM)	"How much do I have in my wallet?"	Understand the value of CFM	Understands that CFM is the key to all wealth foundation
Investment sources	The government	Invest in products or services created by others	Create products and services to sell to middle-class & masses
Expected rate of returns	Get rich quick	10% to 30%	50% to 300% ++
Advisors	Broke family and friends	Financial planner, Accountants, others	Themselves, each others, selected professionals and mentors

24

Why the Rich Get Richer and the Poor Get Poorer?

Robert Kiyosaki, author of *Rich Dad, Poor Dad*, vividly defines asset and liability:

An *asset* is something that puts money in my pocket. A *liability* is something that takes money out of my pocket.

In his book, Kiyosaki said, *"This is really all you need to know. If you want to be rich, simply spend your life buying assets. If you want to be poor or middle-class, spend your life buying liabilities. It's the difference that causes most of the financial struggle on the real world."*

Figure 1.A

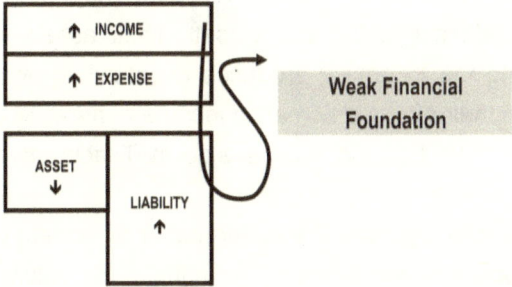

Figure 1.A represents the cash flow of the poor and the middle class. Their income always seems to keep up with their spending and no opportunities to invest on assets. As a result, their liabilities (consumer debts such as loan, mortgage, credit cards, etc.) are higher than their assets.

The poor and the middle class find themselves in a state of constant financial dilemma. Their primary source of income is from their salaries and wages. As their income increase, so do their expenditures and taxes, they are trapped in a rat race.

Figure 1.B

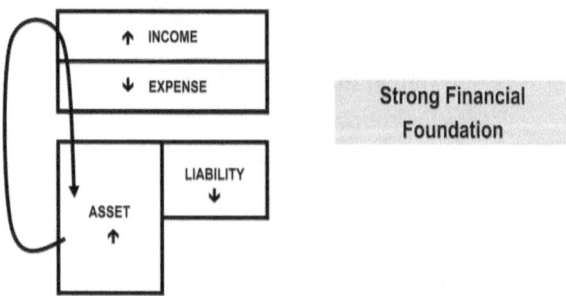

Figure 1.B gives us a clearer picture on how the rich manage their financial resources. Their assets generate an overflow of passive and portfolio income to cover their expenses, with a balance reinvest in the asset itself. Their assets continue to grow making the income it produces eventually grow also. They concentrate their efforts on creating income-generating assets, and keeping their liabilities and expenses down. That is why the rich get richer.

According to Sigmund Freud, the father of modern psychology, there are basically two types of individuals: the failure conscious and the success conscious. The only difference between the two is their manner of thinking. The failure conscious individual harbors a defeatist attitude that reaps failure after failure. Each setback makes him or her to believe that more failures are doomed to come.

If you can confidently move ahead and attains the contrary, you are a success conscious individual. You consistently tell yourself *"I cannot fail!"* and you do not. This theory gives credence to the adage: The rich get richer and the poor get poorer. The rich thinks of creating wealth, while the poor got used with poverty. Each gets exactly what they think.

"Both poverty and riches are the offspring of thought."

- Napoleon Hill

Having or Being

Having immediately flares up our brains if we aspire for something, material or immaterial. By defining your goals in life, wishing for wealth for instance, you tend to strive hard and adapt the ways of the affluent. Others tend to buy fancy houses and luxurious cars and send their kids to schools where the rich send theirs also.

Those aspirations motivate the dreamer to work even harder, to have more debts that the rich does not actually experience. This type of people think that working hard for money and buying things that can make them look rich will make them one. In most cases, it does not. It only makes them more tired.

If you notice, the wannabe's are exhausted. They wear their social mask—the *ego*—to create a self-image which is basically an illusion. They thrive for the approval of others. They are misguided with their ways and fail to remember that they do not have the same mindset as that of a credible wealthy person.

If these wannabes still have the notion of a poor or a middle class and still put-on what the rich does, they would still wind up having what the poor and the middle class have.

Being, on the other hand, is the core of our true nature. It is the mindset of our true self—the *spirit*. When you discover your essential nature of abundance, only then will you realize your potentials and ability to fulfill your dreams. You are the eternal possibility, the immeasurable potential of all that was, is and will be.

Your dreams and desires are like seeds planted on a fertile ground. They are just waiting for the right season to sprout and transform into beautiful flowers and mighty trees. When you come face-to-face with your true self, you will never regret or fear anything. You will realize that the essence of all material wealth lies in your inherent potentials.

You are the Best!

Have you ever wondered how it was when you are in the period of great creation? You are just one of those millions of tiny cells patiently waiting for the divine pairing. Among those participating cells who joined the race, 'you' are the first pair who got stuck with each other. You had won the race. God gave you His spiritual thumbs-up to exist in this world. You have your own purpose and mission in life. Find them.

"Before I formed thee in the belly I knew thee; and before thou camest forth out of the womb I sanctified thee, and I ordained thee." - Jeremiah

In reality, we are divinity in disguise. Our true nature is one of pure spirit, and abundance is our natural state. We are not human beings having spiritual experiences; we are spiritual beings having human experiences. True success, therefore, is the experience of the miraculous. It is the unfolding of the divinity within us. It is the perception and the expression of divinity that guides us wherever we go and whatever we do, not occasionally, but all the time.

Every person is a great miracle. Respect every person you meet along the way; no one knows what he might become in the future. Or you might be that person!

You may not be aware of it, but even before you were born and become the person you are right now, you are already the best!

"What lies behind us and what lies before us are tiny matters compared to what lies within us."

- Ralph Waldo Emerson

📖 The ₱500 Bill

 A well-known resource speaker begins his seminar by waving a ₱500 bill and asking a room full one hundred people, "Who wants this ₱500 bill?" Several hands went up in the air and the speaker crumpled the money, asked once more who wants it, and hands went up in the air again. Then he dropped the money to the floor and stomped it with his feet, making sure it's now tarnished and dirty, but still people wants the ₱500 bill without hesitation. In conclusion, the speaker said that no matter what has been done to the ₱500 bill, people would still want it because its value does not change.

Many times in our lives, we are 'dropped', 'crumpled' and 'stomped at' by the decisions we make and the circumstances that comes our way. We feel as though we are worthless. But no matter what has happened or what will happen to us, we will never lose our true value.

"The true value of a human being can be found in the degree to which he has attained liberation from the self."

- Albert Einstein

You are Worth Millions!

Suppose I am the richest man in town and I own the company you're working for. In one of my business trips, I had a serious accident that severely damaged my eyes. The damage may cause permanent blindness if a transplant is not performed immediately. The only way to regain my normal sight is to find somebody who has the same eye physiology as mine.

Browsing on the company employees' profiles, I came across your medical records and found out that you are the person I am looking for. Your eyes matched mine.

Now, this is my offer: I will pay you ₱1 million if you are willing to grant your eyes for me. No? ₱2 million? ₱5 million? Will you now say yes?

Without a doubt, nobody in his right mind would agree on such proposal. No matter how big the amount is being offered, you will realize within yourself that your real worth is not just millions of pesos—you are priceless!

And if you believe that you are worth more than millions, why persist with your job which gives you only ₱10,000, ₱15,000 or ₱20,000 for a month? Why continue working so hard for a small sum and allow other people to take advantage of your potentials? Reassess yourself and rediscover your true value. Plant your wealth-seed—your potential—in your own field. Redeem the blessed abundance of your life. Do not settle for less of your real value. Earn it because you are worth millions!

"You, yourself, are the 'Money Machine.' You have the ability and opportunity to earn a fortune during your lifetime. See yourself, in your mind's eye, as a creation having unlimited power to build wealth. There is no other creature in existence exactly like you. You are uniquely formed in your mother's womb to make the very best of your God-given attributes, so that you may succeed abundantly in the service of others." - Solomon

"Principles are simple yet powerful models that help us understand how the world works. Principles generate the same result each and every time—no matter where, when, or who uses them. Life is a process of discovering principles—of discovering what works. If you want to make rapid progress, don't fight against principles—flow with them." - Mark Victor Hansen and Robert Allen

Chapter II

PRINCIPLES
OF LEVERAGE

Definition of Leverage

The word *leverage* comes from the old French word *levier* (lever) which means to raise or elevate; to lessen the burden; to delegate; to have the economy of movement; to give a minimum input that achieves maximum results; to multiply time, effort, and money; to do common things which gives exceptional results; or the ability to gain more with less effort and resources.

Examples:

If you use a 5-ft long rod to move a heavy object, the rod is used as a lever. The longer the rod, the easier it can lift and move about an object.

A water pump is a form of a lever. The longer the handle, the lesser effort you need to fill a pail of water.

A pulley is a form of a lever. It minimizes manual labor and allows economy of movement.

A wheel is a form of a lever. It transports heavy objects from one point to another in the easiest manner possible.

Your savings or your time deposit is a form of a lever. It gives you interest income regardless of effort. Money works for you.

A good financial borrowing from the bank or from another entity is a form of a lever. It helps the working and growth capital of one's business venture to be stable.

The human character is a form of a lever. It builds up trust and integrity in the business of life.

"Give me a lever long enough and a fulcrum on which to place it and I shall move the entire earth." - Archimedes

The History of Leverage

The origin of leverage can be traced its roots from the Bible history, in the first creation of all visible things when the Supreme Intelligence mandated the first living man and woman to go and multiply. At the very beginning, God envisioned and authored the Law of Leverage to create and neutralize nature.

Jesus Christ is the prime mover of the Law of Leverage. He asked his disciples, through the lever of His word, to preach the gospel of faith to all people and to all nations. Churches were established and so is the communion of the millions of Christian doctrine believers. That is a perfect example of 'spiritual leverage'.

The powerful force of leverage is applied in almost all successful endeavors in human life: in pursuit of business alliances; in forming a mastermind group; in accumulating wealth; in dealing with our neighbors; and in connecting with our spiritual maker.

The Law of Leverage was discovered and rediscovered because it is inherent to man. This law is the heart of networking and has been existing since time immemorial and will carry on to perpetuity. Like the Law of Gravity, it is absolute and universal because it is a natural law.

We probably came across our own leverage along the way but were not able to harness it. If you see one right now, employ it and benefit a thousand-fold.

The Law of Leverage, if applied appropriately, can lead you to the path of abundant living and to the fulfillment of your desires applying only the least of our efforts.

Work Smarter, Not Harder

Suppose I am to build an artificial fishpond and I need to employ someone to excavate a field measuring one square hectare with a depth of one meter. I will pay you ₱250,000 for the job using your own shovel. If you start digging now, you could probably cover the whole area at the end of the year. I am offering you a large sum because it is my obligation to compensate a laborious job.

Meanwhile, your friend learned of the offer and quickly applied for the same job. He plans to rent a digging machine for ₱50,000 and projects to finish the job in just a week. Do you think he has also done ₱250,000 worth of service? Who worked smart and who worked hard?

What you have just pondered on is an application of the Law of Leverage. The digging machine represents the lever to have the economy of movement and to give a minimum input that can achieve maximum results. Leverage creates speed and simplicity of work or activity performance.

Principle of Least Effort

If you observe nature at work, you will see that least effort is exhausted. Flowers do not even try to bloom, they just bloom. A grass does not even try to grow, it just grows. And so does a bird and a fish, they just fly and swim. Everything works in its intrinsic nature.

It is the nature of the sun to shine; it is the nature of the star to sparkle at night; and it is the nature of a human being to make his dreams unfold into reality.

This concept is also known as the Principle of Least Effort. It is the principle of no resistance or doing less and accomplishing more. It is also the foundation of the Law of Leverage. This principle is utilized when your actions are motivated by love. Nature's sharpness is held together by the power of love.

When you seek power and control over other people, you just waste your energy. When you seek money for your personal gain, you halted the flow of energy and deny the permanence of nature's intelligence. But when your actions are motivated by love, no energy is wasted but doubled instead.

When your actions are motivated by love, your energy multiplies. The surplus energy you accumulated and enjoyed can be a channel in creating what you wish for, including dramatic wealth.

"An integral being knows without going, sees without looking, and accomplishes without doing." - Lao Tzu

📖 The Two Sales Executive

 An owner of a big shoe company in the Philippines plans to construct a factory in South Africa for expansion, thus he sent a Sales Executive to handle the factory construction logistics. The Sales Executive, after conducting a thorough feasibility study, returned to the owner dismayed, saying the project is futile since no one knows how to use shoes. The owner sent another Sales Executive to have a second look, and this executive saw things in a different light, immediately calling the owner. He exclaimed, "Sir, we should put up a shoe factory at once, and teach the huge market here how to wear shoes!"

The two sales executive had seen a similar scenario but assumed a different perspective. The first one settled on the negative aspect while the second viewed the situation in a constructive manner. Seeking for opportunity is a matter of perception.

Opportunityisnowhere

What do you see in OPPORTUNITYISNOWHERE:

Opportunity is NO WHERE or opportunity is NOW HERE.

Suppose I am your employer and I offer you two options on how you can earn your income, what would you choose?

Option 1: ₱250,000 for 30 days of work, or

Option 2: .01 centavo for a day which doubles up
each consecutive day until it reaches the 30th.

Make your choice. (check box)

Table 2.A (The One-Centavo Principle)

Day 1		=	.01
Day 2	.01 x 2	=	.02
Day 3	.02 x 2	=	.04
Day 4	.04 x 2	=	.08
Day 5	.08 x 2	=	.16
Day 6	.16 x 2	=	.32
Day 7	.32 x 2	=	.64
Day 8	.64 x 2	=	1.28
Day 9	1.28 x 2	=	2.56
Day 10	2.56 x 2	=	5.12
Day 11	5.12 x 2	=	10.24
Day 12	10.24 x 2	=	20.48
Day 13	20.48 x 2	=	40.96
Day 14	40.96 x 2	=	81.92
Day 15	81.92 x 2	=	163.84
Day 16	163.84 x 2	=	327.68
Day 17	327.68 x 2	=	655.36
Day 18	655.36 x 2	=	1,310.72
Day 19	1,310.72 x 2	=	2,621.44
Day 20	2,621.44 x 2	=	5,242.88
Day 21	5,242.88 x 2	=	10,485.76
Day 22	10,485.76 x 2	=	20,971.52
Day 23	20,971.52 x 2	=	41,943.04
Day 24	41,943.04 x 2	=	83,886.08
Day 25	83,886.08 x 2	=	167,772.16
Day 26	167,772.16 x 2	=	335,544.32
Day 27	335,544.32 x 2	=	671,088.64
Day 28	671,088.64 x 2	=	1,342,177.28
Day 29	1,342,177.28 x 2	=	2,684,354.56
Day 30	2,684,354.56 x 2	=	<u>5,368,709.12</u>
	TOTAL		₱10,737,418.23

Is not that an amazing figure? At first glance, you would probably choose Option 1 but taking a closer look at Option 2 would boggle your mind with several digit numbers that can actually send out a much larger amount of income. The secret behind earning this much at a shorter period of time lies in the Principle of Multiplier Effect which can also be attributed to the Law of Leverage.

If you learn to understand and adapt the Law of Leverage in your wealth-building plan, this can lead you to financial and time freedom with less difficulty. This principle is the main reason why most network marketers earn more than those traditional workers and employees; they have discovered the most important factor in attaining wealth.

Duplication is the name of the game. Duplicate yourself through other people and you can easily multiply your sources of income beyond your expectations. Let this be your guiding principle: Learn by heart how to leverage your time, money and effort, and find a person who can do the task similar to your capacity.

Time Lever

Our time is very limited. Each one of us has only 24 hours to spare for our daily activities. For a day, we work for at least 8 hours. Another 8 hours is spent for sleep or rest and the remaining 8 more hours is for leisure and other activities.

In the Philippine setting, the minimum wage for a typical employee ranges from ₱10,000 to ₱15,000 for a month. If you are earning ₱12,000 monthly and you work eight hours for each day, you are basically making ₱400 per day or ₱50 in an hour. The question is, "How can you increase your income without disrupting or leaving your present job?"

How much you earn for an hour, for a day, or for a month are relevant. Making big money lies in the creation and multiplication of your Time-Making Money (time lever) through other people in your organization. You may not know it but the answer to your earlier question is well-hidden in your eight hours a day.

Table 2.B

Hours of work	Rate per hour	Income per day
8	₱50	₱400
12	₱50	₱600
20	₱50	₱1,000
50	₱50	₱2,500
100	₱50	₱5,000
500	₱50	₱25,000
1,000	₱50	₱50,000
2,000	₱50	₱100,000
5,000	₱50	₱250,000
10,000 etc.	₱50	₱500,000 etc.

Referring to Table 2.B, note that the rate per hour is constant to ₱50 only. The increase in the income per day is proportionate to the increase of the time inputs. Therefore, more hours of work means greater income outputs that can be generated. But how can you apply this principle in real life?

Network Marketing is the only business system which conforms to Time Compounding and acquires a desirable result. You can start the business by introducing your organization to interesting individuals and invite them to be your business partners or counterparts. These new partners may also invite more others and produce their own counterparts and so on. Your time then is compounded and their time becomes your time, and it would later trickle down to everybody else in the organization.

If you are connected to a network of 1,000 people in your organization, each contributing an hour per day (making it 1,000 hours per day), it can earn you as much as ₱50,000 for a day. And what if these business builders work two hours or more for each day, then your income will soon be exponential!

This wealth-building process is also known as leveraging through Other People's Time (OPT). Do not be surprised if you hear about ordinary people earning as much as ₱50,000; ₱100,000; ₱200,000; ₱300,000; ₱500,000 or even more than ₱1 million per month in this industry. The secret lies in the multiplication of their time-making money.

Bill Gates, founder of Microsoft and one of the richest man, has an estimated net worth of $77.1 billion as of 2014, according to Forbes magazine. That assuming that he worked on every business day since Microsoft was founded in 1975, for 8 hours a day, he could have earned around $250,000 per hour. His secret? He multiplies his Time-Making Money through his thousands of employees and associates in all his businesses and investments that generates profits and passive/residual income.

Can you now visualize how the stated principles are incorporated with the network marketing business? If you do congratulations! You have unveiled the most important key in wealth building, the Law of Leverage.

Think again. If you share this principle with your immediate concerns and invite them to be your business partners, the effect of exponential growth in your income will surely amaze you.

What Do These Billionaires Have in Common?

Bill Gates	Microsoft Corp.
Carlos Slim Helu	America Movil
Warren Buffet	Berkshire Hathaway
Ray Kroc	Mc Donalds Corp.
Harland Sanders	KFC
Henry Ford	Ford Motors
Ted Turner	CNN Network

Larry Ellison	Oracle Corp.
Michael Dell	Dell Computers
Mark Zuckerberg	Facebook
Jeff Beroz	Amazon.com
John Gokongwei	JG Summit Phils.
Manny Villar	C & P Homes Phils.
Henry Sy	SM Shoe Mart
Lucio Tan	Fortune Tobacco
Tony Tan Caktiong	Jollibee Corp.
Eugenio Lopez Jr.	ABS-CBN Network
Tan Yu	Fuga Int'l Group Phils.
Jaime Zobel de Ayala	Ayala Corp.
George Ty	Metro Bank Phils.

They mind their own business and practice the Law of Leverage!

The Value of Your Dreams

Education for your children	₱6,000,000
A decent home	₱4,000,000
A fine vehicle	₱2,000,000
A reasonable savings and investments	₱5,000,000
A great tour and adventure	₱2,000,000
A good service and act of charity	₱2,000,000
A better health care and insurance	₱3,000,000
Legacy for loved ones	₱6,000,000
Total average value of your dream	**₱30,000,000**

How much is your present income? _____

Can you achieve your life dreams with your present income 5 years from now? 10 years from now? How?

"Dreams are the seedlings of realities." - James Allen

"Dream big dreams. Only big dreams have the power to move men's soul." - Marcus Aurelius

It's Time to Reclaim Your Dreams

The secret of a self-made millionaire is simple: They dream big dreams! Allow yourself to dream and envision the kind of life you would like to have. You must have a dream if you want one to come true.

Imagine that you have no limitations on what you can be, have, or do in life; that you have all the time, money, friends, resources, and everything else you want to achieve in life. Then think again: If your potentials are unlimited, what kind of life can you provide for you and your family?

Project your life 5 years ahead, imagine that your life is perfect in every aspect, and ask yourself the following questions:

What is it like?

What do you do for a living?

Where do you work?

How much money do you earn?

How much money do you save in the bank?

What kind of lifestyle do you have?

Now, step out of the future, look back to where you are today, and ask yourself again:

What will you do to achieve your dreams?

What can you do to succeed?

What type of opportunities would you look for?

Whatever it is, take the first step today. If you can dream it, do it!

Here is Your Chance!

Who makes more money, the person who owns the company or an employee who works for him? The owner, of course. Your boss' job is not to make you rich but to make sure that you receive your paycheck. The truth is it is your job to become rich—if you wanted to.

My friend, you now have the opportunity to own and mind your own business and to decide how much money you can earn. Do you want to remain an employee and let your boss decide your earnings, or do you wish to start your own business and be the boss by becoming an independent entrepreneur now.

"Man has the power to transform his thoughts into physical reality; man can dream and make his dreams come true. Cherish your visions and your dreams, as they are the children of your soul; the blueprints of your ultimate achievements." - Napoleon Hill

Bread or Diamond

 The principle of bread and diamond tells that each of us has a limited source of income and how we spend it is up to us. Each peso in our pocket has the power to make us richer or poorer. We may spend our precious money on bread or diamond, or a combination of both.

By bread, I mean spending on consumables (necessities of life) and other items that depreciate and lower its value over time. By diamond, I mean investing on valuables—*real assets*—that appreciate its value over a period of time like shares in stocks and bonds, marketable securities or venturing into a viable business (conventional, franchise, or network marketing), real estate, precious gems and other income-generating properties.

The more you spend on bread, the lesser there will be for diamonds. You can choose to invest on things that go either up or down in value. If you invest wisely today, then your diamonds will generate enough income to buy all the bread you will ever need and want for tomorrow. But if you spend all your money on bread today, you might not have any left to buy diamonds for tomorrow. Prosperity does not come from what you earn, it comes from what you do with what you have.

The doctrine of *financial literacy* is, "Pay yourself first." A part of all you earn is yours to keep and to invest to produce more of its kind; to spend less on what you earn and invest the difference.

Wrong : INCOME — EXPENSE = SAVING
Right : INCOME — SAVING = EXPENSE

Most of us has a mindset of earning our income, spend it, and what is left is put into safety. That is the hard way to multiply your personal wealth. To build up your personal wealth save a reasonable sum, say 10-30% for investment, and the rest to be spent for your legitimate needs and expenses. Practice a good system of budgeting and live within your means.

Remember that saving is actually an expense; however, an expense that will buy you a diamond—your future prosperity.

"The secret is to spend what you have left after saving, instead of saving what you have left after spending."

- Frank Newman

See Yourself as an Entrepreneur

Highly productive people envision themselves to be an effective entrepreneur. If you are one of them, you must possess the entrepreneurial mentality: highly-independent, responsible, self-reliant, and decisive.

Instead of waiting for things to happen, you initiate for things to happen. Be proactive—a habit practiced by most achievers. They believe that, as human beings, they are responsible for their own lives. Our behavior is a function or our decisions and not of our conditions. We are responsible for making things happen.

We are the architect of our own destiny. Envision yourself as the "President and C.E.O. (Chief Executive Officer)" of your own life totally in charge of your physical health, your financial well-being, your career, your relationship, your lifestyle, your home, your car, and every element of your existence. This is the mindset of a self-made millionaire.

"Whatever the mind of man can conceive and believe it can achieve." - Napoleon Hill

The Better Hamburger

 Do you remember how a Jollibee hamburger tastes like? If you are given sufficient time can you develop a better hamburger than Jollibee? Probably you would say, "Yes!"

Now, this is the second question: Can you create a better business system than Jollibee has?

That is where the big difference lies. A majority may welcome the idea of producing a better hamburger but only a few can cope to establish a powerful business system. Just the same, thousands of people can create a better burger but only Jollibee has the system that can serve millions of hamburgers.

If you want to learn a distinctive business system, visit a Jollibee store and observe how their system works. When you enter the store, warm greetings welcome you: "Good Morning, Sir/Ma'am. Welcome to Jollibee... Thank you for coming..." Observe the service and the way they handle certain tasks, from the managers down to the crew.

Take note also of the following: who raises their meat products; what bakeshop bakes their buns; how do they make the thousands of kilos of French Fries that taste the same all over its franchise stores nationwide; and the commercial TV ads with their famous Jollibee mascot.

Then include the investors and brokers who finance their operations. If you can execute the same picture, then you have a good chance to belong in the Business and Investment Quadrant— the favorable paths toward financial freedom.

Tony Tan Caktiong created a regular product. He just developed it and built a powerful system around it. The same goes for a network marketing business, which is a business similar to Jollibee. All you have to do is find the right companies with a strong business system that can help you leverage your time and effort in building your financial net worth.

Why People Join the Network Marketing Business?

Statistics say that the primary reasons why people from different walks of life join this business were accounted on one of the motivating factors below:

Extra or Supplementary Income
Financial Freedom
Establish Own Business
More Spare Time
Helping Others
Early Retirement
Leave a Legacy
Personal Development
Meeting New People

How about you? Before answering the following questions, please spend at least 5 to 10 minutes to ponder:

What is your number one priority?
Why did you choose it?
Why is it important to you?

What are the consequences of not having that opportunity?
Why would that worry you?

(Adapted from *Questions are the Answers* by Allan Pease)

*"Leverage Marketing is all about building relationship;
it's all about changing lives; it's all about free life."*

- Rane A. Panaligan

Return on Investment (ROI)

If you have ₱10,000 in your possession right now and you wish
to invest it in something that will earn you more of its kind, which
investment option would you prefer among the three:

(1) Bank; (2) Conventional; (3) Network Marketing

R.O.I.

1. Bank (₱10,000 x 3% p.a.) = ₱300/yr. or ₱25/mo.
2. Conventional business = 10% - 30% profit
3. Network Marketing (₱10,000 investment) = Freedom
    a. Financial Freedom (Stable source of residual income)
    b. Personal Freedom (More quality time with family)
    c. Helping other people to do the same
    What would you choose?

*"In 1984 20% of new millionaires came from Network
Marketing. By 1994 it was 50%. It's predicted that by 2004
and forward, 70-80% of new millionaires will come from the
booming Network Marketing industry."* - IRS (U.S.) Statistics

Marketing Channel of Distribution

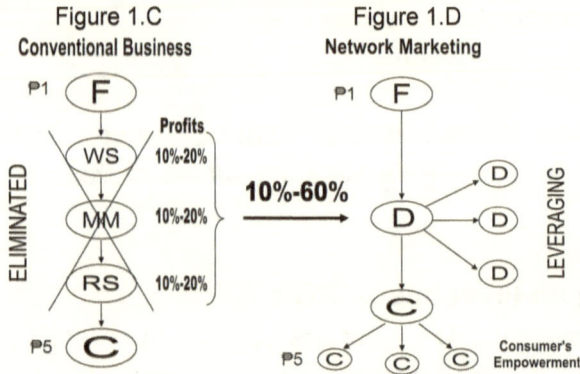

Figure 1.C
Conventional Business

Figure 1.D
Network Marketing

In a conventional business, a product which comes straight from a factory is transported to *wholesaler*, then distributed to a *middleman*, down to the *retailer* and finally to the *consumer*. Normally, this business system employs a three-channel of distribution.

The network marketing system, on the other hand, uses only a one-channel of distribution: From the factory, to the distributors, and down to the consumers.

Figure 1.C shows that a product originally costs ₱1 but by the time it reaches the consumer, it already costs ₱5. The price increment is due to various overheads, example: warehousing, insurance, salaries and wages, rent, advertising, etc. incurred during operations plus the average profit of 10-20% gained by the wholesaler, the middleman and, the retail stores.

Figure 1.D illustrates otherwise. A network marketing business eliminates unnecessary channels and creates a legitimate shortcut to the distribution process. This allows the distributors to link directly the factory and the consumer through word-of-mouth advertising. This system can spare the entrepreneur the advertising and media expenses.

If you are a distributor in a network marketing business, your significant sales and efforts can be remunerated in form of discounts, rebates, commissions, bonuses, royalties, and other benefits. The distributor now becomes the wholesaler, the middleman, and the retailer rolled into one, and can consolidate all the 10-60% profits and other benefits, which is contrary to a conventional business distribution channel of marketing.

You can also build and establish your own chain of distributors under a network or organization and earn you more royalties and residual income. Yourself and the distributors in your own network becomes the walking factory and stores of a network marketing company. This will establish a mutual leveraging or *bayanihan* and will allow you and the rest of your network to earn more by employing least effort.

Consumer's Empowerment

The three kinds of business systems are as follows: (1) Conventional; (2) Franchise; and (3) Network Marketing. Among the three, the most favorable system to start your venture is via network marketing. You only need a very minimal capital that can gain you a long-term source of residual income.

Consumer's empowerment is a great privilege and an advantage if you are associated with a Network Marketing business. In a conventional business, example: groceries, sari-sari stores, convenience stores, etc., you seldom get significant discounts unlike in an network marketing business; you do not just get big discounts and rebates, you can also create your life's dreams by creating a business of your own. By patronizing and endorsing a product, you can acquire a prolonged source of a residual income.

The People's Franchise

McDonald's, KFC, Jollibee, Pizza Hut, Starbucks, and Burger King are just some of the leading franchises here in the Philippines and abroad. These fast-food companies acquire more and more franchises or interconnecting outlets to serve their line of various quality products to their respective patrons.

A franchise is another form of a business system wherein its head outlet sells their business concept and system to a group of qualified business operators for an upfront franchise fee and royalties.

On the average, the set-up capital of well-known franchise systems ranges from ₱5 million to ₱30 million or more per store while a small-scale franchise may cost you from ₱100,000 to ₱1 million per contract.

A network marketing business also operates as a traditional franchise but on a micro-level capacity. This business is easy to set up. You can establish your own outlet or franchise for your immediate concerns and potential business counterparts and enjoy the same income benefits without incurring too many overhead and operating expenses.

The network marketing business is an alternative franchise system, has a very minimal start-up capital that normally ranges from ₱1,000 to ₱50,000 only. You can easily recover your capital investment (R.O.I.) on a shorter period. Like a typical franchise, you can also expand your network marketing business by having walking stores in different places.

Another good feature of this system is you can do it home--based. You will be your own boss and experience more time freedom than any other ordinary employees and professionals. By applying the most important key in wealth creation, the law of leverage, you can achieve a maximum output from your minimum input by multiplying your time and effort through other people.

The Law of Leverage can accelerate the exponential growth in your own network and allow you to have an unlimited source of residual income. In the Network Marketing business, you will encounter several successful ordinary people earning extraordinary income.

If you can visualize the kind of lifestyle this business has to offer (which is definitely achievable), you must work your way with a completely new positive outlook and attitude. Once you see the potential, you will never quit. Think of all the pleasure you can provide for your loved ones. Let it inspire you to give it your all to succeed.

"When the product is right, you don't have to be a great marketer." - Lee Iacocca

The Credibility of Network Marketing Industry

The Network Marketing business will be the wave of the 21st century. Back in June 1999, Network Marketing or Multi-Level Marketing (M.L.M.) was introduced in Ateneo de Manila and became a part of their curriculum as a 3-unit subject. The Asian Institute of Management (A.I.M.) also offers a 2-week marketing strategy course on network marketing concepts and principles.

In the United States, schools like the University of Illinois and the University of Houston teaches Network Marketing subjects as part of their curriculum, too.

Below are relevant facts and figures on the development and progress of the Network Marketing and Direct Selling industries:

In 1998, these industries generated an $80 billion retail sales worldwide including $22 billion in the United States, $26 billion in Japan, $4 billion in Brazil, $3.6 billion in Germany, $2.1 billion in Mexico, $1.8 billion in the United Kingdom, $1.7 billion in Taiwan, $1.6 billion in Canada, and over $1.5 billion each in Australia, France, and Argentina.

Statistics in the global market shows that there are about 33 million network marketing and direct selling associates as of 1998, including the 9.3 million in the United States, 2.6 million in Indonesia, 2.5 million in Japan and Thailand, 2.4 million in Taiwan, 1.8 million in both Brazil and Malaysia and 1.3 million in both Canada and Mexico. In the Philippines, an estimate of 1 million people directly and indirectly participates in the same business.

The statistics above confirms that the Network Marketing business is a fast-growing industry that can be considered as an alternative medium for wealth creation on the 21st century. We are now in the great period of 'individualism'—the age of the knowledge worker.

The 3 Pillars of Network Marketing

The Network Marketing business is the only business system that maximizes leveraging, exponential growth, and residual income. The combination of the three will efficiently deliver synergy and exceptional performance for this kind of business system.

LEVERAGING
EXPONENTIAL GROWTH
RESIDUAL INCOME

Unfortunately, the majority of the population often misunderstands these principles; it is the main reason why several people and aspirants failed in the network marketing business. If one cannot fully comprehend leveraging, exponential growth and residual income, a transfer of information is improbable.

This misapprehension can be attested by what our educational system has trained us to be—conformists: "To do what others tell us to do and to look for a job after we complete a college degree." Never mind if you cannot put up your own business. Many people claim they would like to be their own boss but only a small percentage possess the burning desire for success and are willing to risk their comfort zones.

Most people are afraid of failures. Others are satisfied with their jobs. However, if you are among millions of people who yearn for greater economic freedom, you must be able to understand the three principles to achieve lasting success in the business of life:

Leveraging

Success of a person or success in business may be derived from leveraging. Leveraging your time through other people's efforts can dramatically increase your income and gain you time freedom.

Undoubtedly, in most traditional businesses, the only ones who benefit from this leverage are the owners or stockholders of business entities. Loyal and hardworking employees do most of the hard work but are not fairly compensated.

In network marketing business, everyone involved has an equal opportunity to own a business by investing only a fraction of his or her time and money. Even those from the conventional and franchise business can involve themselves. They only have to take a little from their major investments to join network marketing.

Several talented people find it difficult to grasp this concept and hardly give this concept a try. The idea here is your income would not be dependent on one person only. In a conventional business, if a person or an associate gets sick, injured, pass away, quit working or decided to go on long vacation, the issuance of an income could stop. But if your income is produced by the *activities of many*, that business is more reliable.

In network marketing, if something unexpected happens to one or more of your business partners, it will only have a minor effect on the total production and your residual income will continue to flow. That is how the people who makes use of this concept live the lifestyle they choose and get paid even while on vacation.

That is one of the many advantages of leveraging your time and is the main reason why several high-income professionals flock into network marketing. In this industry, you will not only have the financial freedom you desire but also the time freedom to enjoy.

Always ask yourself, "Where is my lever?"

"I would rather earn 1% out of the effort of 100 people than to earn 100% of my own effort." - Jean Paul Getty

Exponential Growth

The best example of exponential growth is shown in table 2.A (the one-centavo principle). If you start with a centavo for a day and double itself each consecutive day, the result will be dramatic. The same table can also show you how a network marketing system works.

If I can teach you this principle, I have doubled myself. If we each teach someone else, we have doubled into four and as this activity goes on and on, it can produce an amazing result in a relatively shorter period, just as the one centavo has.

Residual Income

Residual Income is the recurring stream of income that continuously flows in your account even after you have fulfilled your share of time and effort. It is like making money while you are sleeping. This type of income is a one-time effort that produces a lifetime source and flow of income. There are several ways to produce a residual income but many people are misinformed, have never thought about or have not been exposed to it.

How many percentage of your income is residual? Leverage your time and effort to increase your residual; it is the best source of all types of income. Successful authors, composers, artists, insurance agents, and network builders produce this type of income.

The best example of a passive residual income is the interest earned on money saved in the bank, dividend received on investments, or rentals from real estate properties. All these income can credit to your account without having to invest any more time and effort on your part to produce it.

The concept of the residual income is incorporated in the network marketing system. Involvement in this type of business means enjoying the benefits of a residual or lifetime income.

If you understand and believe in the righteousness of the three empowering principles, without a doubt, you can succeed in this industry. If you are more than willing to teach leveraging, exponential growth and residual income to a few others, the result may profoundly surprise you.

"One of the most noble of all profession is Network Marketing because you teach other people how to achieve their dreams and help them to make a difference in their lives." - The Networkpreneur

The 4-Year Versus 40-Year Plan

A financial condition is not the primary requisite to get involved in network marketing business. Whether you are a professional or not, you are 'in' as long as you can work with full commitment, discipline and perseverance. If you believe in what you can do, you can achieve your objectives at the earliest possible time.

₱10,000 per month x 12 months
= ₱120,000 x **40 years** = ₱4.8 million

₱100,000 per month x 12 months
= ₱1,200,000 x **4 years** = ₱4.8 million

Years saved = **36**

By involving in a network marketing business, you will be able to distinguish between *small money* and *big money*. If you are currently earning ₱10,000 per month and continue to earn the same exact amount in the succeeding 40 years, you can accumulate a total of ₱4.8 million worth of your income for a lifetime. At first glance, ₱4.8 million is big money but then you realize that all of your daily expenses will also come from your ₱10,000 monthly income. Too small or nothing will be left for saving.

On the other hand, if you are earning ₱100,000 a month in your network marketing business and continuously earn it until you reach ₱4.8 million, note that you need to spend only 4 solid years to come up with the same result and saved 36 working years!

You can retire young and wealthy and enjoy a far better life. You can recreate your destiny and noble dreams again and again to fulfill your highest purpose of living. So, why spend 40 years of hard work if you can achieve your life's dreams in just 4 years?

"In 1989, when Berlin wall came down and the World Wide Web (www) went up, the rules of the world had changed forever. According to many economic historians, that's when the Industrial Age ended, and the Information Age began. In the Industrial Age, the rules were that if you work hard, your company and the government would take care of you. In the Information Age, the rules are different: The new rules say, you had better planning to take care of yourself. How? Starting now, by investing in your own Network Marketing business." - Robert Kiyosaki

"Anyone who moves into Network Marketing with excitement, commitment and hard work has given himself the basic ingredients to succeed. This is what is so fantastic about this opportunity–just about anyone can succeed if he starts with right attitude and adopts the right approach. It is the finest opportunity available to every ordinary man." - Ong Hoch Siew

Three Kinds of Income

Earned Income

This type of income is usually earned by rendering one's productivity either its nature is professional, clerical, industrial, or agricultural. This source of income is called *earned income* (also known as the fixed, linear or active income), which comes in the form of salaries, wages, and professional fees.

Passive Income

Compound Interest and compound growth is the source of this type of income. They come in form of rent from real estate properties, residual income and royalties (sales of books, network builders' income, music, compositions, inventions, etc.), interest from bank savings and time deposits, net profit from a business and many others of the same kind.

Portfolio Income

This type of income chiefly comes from paper investments such as stocks, bonds, trust funds, marketable securities, and other related income-producing assets.

When our parents tell us to study hard, get good grades, and look for a stable job—we are talking about earned income. It is like planting a mongo plant; you need to plant the seeds again and again to have a good harvest.

But when smart parents tell their children to study hard, graduate and learn to manage a business of your own and let the money work for you instead of you working for the money, we are talking here of residual income—passive and portfolio. It is like planting a mango tree; one-time planting, lifetime harvest.

How Much is Your Net Worth?

Our main goal in venturing in any kind of business system is to adapt a better leverage to achieve exceptional net worth or net asset equity. To secure financial freedom, it is necessary for us to learn first the fundamentals of *Financial Literacy*—the ability to read numbers. In any business venture, *Accounting* is used when communicating in numbers; it is the universal language in any business. It communicates relevant financial information of business entity as a basis of informed economic decisions.

The first basic equation is,

(Equation 1)
ASSETS = LIABILITIES + CAPITAL

To obtain your Net Worth, deduct your liabilities from your assets. Thus,

(Equation 2)
ASSETS - LIABILITIES = NET WORTH

From Equation 2, we can now distinguish an asset from a liability. In non-technical language, *Asset* is defined as any monetary value that increases your Net Worth while a *Liability* is that monetary value that reduces your Net Worth.

A significant increment on your net worth can be attained if you minimize or decrease your expenditures and focus more on procuring income-generating assets to produce more of its kind. Hence,

(Equation 3)
ASSETS - LIABILITIES = NETWORTH
(Increase)   (Decrease)   (Increase)

If you were able to understand those three basic equations, congratulations! Your Financial Quotient (F.Q.) is now in progress.

F.Q. is the ability to read and understand relevant monetary data and figures. When it comes to money, it is not how much you make that counts, but how much you keep and invest that savings to generate more of its kind.

Therefore, to apply a better lever for your net worth, you must focus in increasing your assets and in decreasing your liabilities. It is very important to live within your means and at the same time to expand your means. Control your expenditures and invest your savings and surplus earnings to produce a residual income.

To better acquaint yourself with assets and liabilities, you must instill in your mind the two rules in net worth building:

Rule # 1

Learn to distinguish an asset from a liability. Focus on creating and buying income-producing assets to generate a passive or a portfolio income.

Rule # 2

Always practice the Law of Leverage.

If you are considering a feasible business to start, a venture in network marketing is highly recommended to secure a substantial net worth. This business provides more privileges and distinctive opportunities for your personal net worth.

There is no need for employees, no rent, no electricity bills, and no dress code. It requires lesser capital, lesser overhead, lesser taxes, lesser legalities, and even lesser risks. You are the boss and you can acquire time freedom while earning an unlimited source of income—just leverage your time and effort.

If you already have a solid source of stream of income from this business system, you can now create an investment portfolio and other feasible entrepreneurial businesses. Just follow the two net worth building rules, take calculated risk, seek wise advice and consistently educate yourself and widen your horizons to discover more opportunities in increasing your net worth. Leverage, leverage, and leverage more!

"Financial success requires a man to have a plan for savings, as well as for spending, enabling him to create a surplus that wisely employ to bring financial freedom for the future." - Solomon

How Strong is Your Wealth?

In minding your own business, one of your most crucial task as an independent entrepreneur, whether you are engaged in conventional, franchise, or network marketing business system, is to effectively calculate and monitor your wealth ratio on a monthly basis to properly administer the financial/economic aspect of your life. The formula is:

<u>**PASSIVE INCOME + PORTFOLIO INCOME**</u>
TOTAL MONTHLY EXPENSES

The objective of calculating your wealth ratio is to have your passive and portfolio income equal or greater than your total monthly expenses. The moment you have a ratio of one is to one or more (>1:1), it indicates that you have increased your financial capacity to live a better life and start to improve your wealth base. On the other hand, if your wealth ratio is less than one (<1:1), it implies that you are still in a financial dilemma and your cash flow does not meet your basic life standard.

To illustrate, if your combined monthly income from passive and portfolio is ₱50,000 and your total monthly expenses is ₱20,000 your wealth ratio is 2.5:1. This signifies that for every peso expense, your income can cover it by ₱2.50 or 2.5 times of your expenses. There is a surplus income of ₱1 at .50 centavos for every peso expense.

Similarly, if your combined passive and portfolio income for the month is ₱30,000 and your expenses is ₱50,000 you have a wealth ratio of 0.6:1. This indicates that for every peso expense, your income can cover it up to .60 centavos or 60%.

The key in improving your wealth ratio is to regularly monitor and increase your passive and portfolio income by increasing your means to earn more instead of acquiring more expenses. The moment you decide to make the passive and portfolio income a part of your financial habit and discipline yourself in building it, your life will change and be more fulfilling. This is the path in maintaining a strong wealth foundation.

"Leverage is the key to great wealth." - Robert Kiyosaki

📖 Extra Income has More Value

Crispin and Basilio are both distributors, and one afternoon, Crispin bursts into the office, exclaiming the best thing has ever happened to him when he received his bonus check of ₱4,500. Basilio couldn't understand why he was so excited, and after Crispin said that his take home pay is only ₱9,000 per month, Basilio said it's just 50% of his salary. Crispin explained that each month, after tending to all his obligations—rent, food, debts, and other bills—an amount of ₱450 is left as his personal spending money. The ₱4,500 bonus check is from his MLM business, and it increases his spending money by ten times.

Not everyone needs a big amount of check to gain pleasure in this business. The concept of leverage in a network marketing business will let you appreciate modest increments in your spending income. Never underestimate the value of the extra income you can earn from this business, for next time, more will come to you.

"Doing common things exceptionally well will determine your capacity to build great wealth." - Rane A.Panaligan

Spare Tire Principle

Whenever you drive a car, you are carrying a spare tire, right. Are you expecting a flat tire? Of course not! You carry a spare tire just in case you have a flat tire. You just want to be prepared when hitting the road to reach your destination without further delay.

Apply this principle for your income to have a constant flow. You should not be contented to one source of income. You should create and develop spare sources of residual income (passive at portfolio) so that even you lose your job, getting sick, or a company shutdown—your income never stop like a running water in the spring, continuous, and overflowing.

"Invest your money in foreign trade, and one of these days you will make a profit. Put your investment in several places—many places even—because you never know what kind of bad luck you are going to have in this world." – Solomon

Figure 1.E

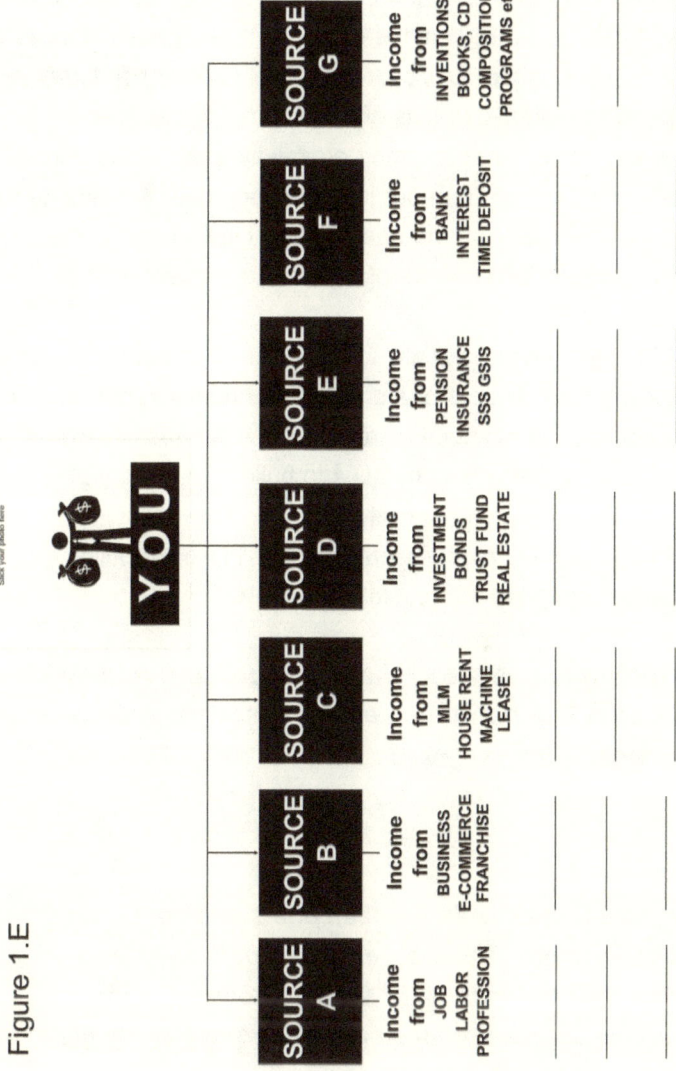

Stick your photo here

YOU

SOURCE A	SOURCE B	SOURCE C	SOURCE D	SOURCE E	SOURCE F	SOURCE G
Income from	Income from	Income from	Income from	Income from	Income from	Income from
JOB LABOR PROFESSION	BUSINESS E-COMMERCE FRANCHISE	MLM HOUSE RENT MACHINE LEASE	INVESTMENT BONDS TRUST FUND REAL ESTATE	PENSION INSURANCE SSS GSIS	BANK INTEREST TIME DEPOSIT	INVENTIONS BOOKS, CD COMPOSITION PROGRAMS etc.

Multiple Sources of Income (MSI)

Do you have a Multiple Sources of Income (M.S.I.) flowing in your resources at this very moment? In this economic world where no job or business is secured or stable, it is advisable for an individual to have an MSI. Almost 50% of the companies who once belonged to Fortune 500 during the 1980's are no longer in operation today, and that can be converted to a loss of more than 5 million jobs.

The key point is not ensuring ourselves a job but to ascertain that we are not cut-off from our income resources. Nowadays, it is a great risk if you depend on one source of income only. You must create a portfolio of streams of income to prepare you for life's consequences.

MSI means having multiple sources of income without acquiring an extra job. Each source of a cash flow increasing your net worth is independent of the other. Figure 1.E shows a perfect layout of the MSI principle, which is synonymous to building a good four-legged foundation for a house for stability.

MSI is one of the most essential factors in wealth-building often acquired by financially successful individuals.

"The difference between the rich, poor and middle class is leverage. The difference between savers and investors is leverage." - Robert Kiyosaki

My M.S.I.

I realize that I need more than one source of Income.
I choose a new and wiser financial path.
It is called the wisdom of Multiple Sources of Income.
Multiple Sources of Income are pouring into my life,
and from all over the world.

- One Minute Millionaire

"In this era of fast changing technology, there is no certificate, diploma, or degree which can see you through a lifetime employment. Knowledge and skills get outdated with rapid changes in technologies." - Lee Kuan Yew

The Millionaire's Mind Account

Before you can earn the first million and manifest it in your bank account, you must deposit it first to your internal bank account to become a reality. This account is called the 'Millionaire's Mind Account'. Remember that everything is created twice—the financial blueprint (mind creation) and the financial reality (physical creation). Without the blueprint, there would be no concrete reality.

You should learn and adapt first the irrefutable qualities of the millionaires. You must consistently cultivate abundant mentality. Focus your attention on creating a higher level of wealth consciousness, 'mind your own business', and practice the Law of Leverage. If you do, 90% percent of your wealth building process is already assured, the remaining 10% is just methods and procedures.

The mind, if properly trained in wealth awareness is the most powerful leverage in the attainment of any financial goals in the business of life. Based on research, there are twenty-one most common qualities practice by self-made millionaires.

They are:
(Please check the box that applies to you)

☐ Dreamer (visionary)
☐ Entrepreneurial (innovator)
☐ Intuitional (creative)
☐ Proactive (responsible)
☐ Futurist (possibility thinker)
☐ Leader
☐ Goal Oriented
☐ Focus Direction

- ☐ Purpose Driven
- ☐ Passionate
- ☐ Committed
- ☐ Decisive
- ☐ Disciplined
- ☐ Determined
- ☐ Hardworking
- ☐ Result Oriented
- ☐ Systematic
- ☐ Emphatic
- ☐ Adaptable
- ☐ Learner
- ☐ Giver

"The Law of Income: You will be paid in direct proportion to the value you deliver according to the marketplace."

- T. Harv Eker

The 7 Money Habits of Truly Rich People
They value it

The rich treats money with great respect and does not waste it. They know that money is a financial seed that can create wealth and can be used as lever to achieve time and financial freedom.

They make it

The rich fabricates the money. They work to learn. The sharper their mind, the easier for them to project enormous earning possibilities at a shorter period of time.

They manage it

The rich understands and applies effective Cash Flow Management (C.F.M.). They practice a precise budgetary plan for every peso in their possession.

They save it

The rich believes that a part of what they earn is theirs to keep, which is fundamental for financial literacy. They know that a small amount can turn itself into a substantial sum.

They invest it

The rich believes in the law of the harvest. They plant the wealth-seed, cultivate it, and allow it to leverage more of its kind.

They shield it

The rich safeguards their wealth tightly. They believe that financial wealth is measured not by how much they earn but how much they keep. They insure and preserve their wealth with great caution.

They share it

The rich practice the principle of blessed giving. They share what they have open-heartedly. Giving is a money multiplier that adds value to their prosperity a thousand fold. They believe that there is a time for accumulation and a time for distribution. The ultimate purpose of financial wealth is to help others find their own.

"Wealth is when small efforts produce big results. Poverty is when big efforts produce small results."

- George Davis

"Riches do not respond to wishes. They respond only to definite plans, backed by definite desires, through constant persistence." - Napoleon Hill

The 7 Most Important Reasons Why You Should Get Involved in Networkpreneurship

The ability to control your life

Who controls your financial life? Nobody wants to become slave of others. Deep in our hearts, we want to take control of our lives. Individually and collectively, we want freedom from all kinds of lack and struggle—financially, mentally, emotionally and spiritually.

If you don't like the result of your present occupation, change your reality and find ways on how to change the direction of your life to achieve the lifestyle you like and to enjoy the life you want. Whatever you choose and believe, you will become. Own your life.

A current business trend

The 21st century economy is characterized by speed and power of network. Whether you like it or not, you are involved. Your job is to position yourself in this 'golden opportunity' already in front of us. Your time has come to become a networkpreneur—the Exponential Entrepreneur (E^2).

This branch of entrepreneurship is unique of its class. Venturing in this kind of business model will give you the following distinctive benefits and possibilities:

- Unlimited source of residual income (passive at portfolio).

- A business with no boundaries and unlimited market expansion worldwide.

- You are the boss. You have the total freedom to operate your business at your own pace.

- No entry barrier. No academic or PhD requirements to succeed in this venture.

- Competition is not the way. The faster they copy your business, the faster it will explode.

- You are setting-up an alternative franchise model with minimal investment and overhead.

- This business will lead you to a diamond lifestyle.

- Industry growth: 1980 - $10 billion; 1992 - $40 billion: 1996 - $70 billion; 2009 - $100 billion, 2012 - $167 billion; 2014 onward - $ trillion industry.

The focal question: Am I going to be one of the people who just observe the explosion of networkpreneurship over the next decade or am I going to be the one of the people who supports to make it explode and gain residual income in the process?

Your ability to leverage and multiply your time-making money through others

If there is one principle in this book that you must learn by heart and master in depth, it's the Law of Leverage—the key to exponential wealth. This principle is the heart of networkpreneurship a.k.a. Network Marketing or Multi-Level Marketing (M.L.M.). Without this principle, the idea of financial and time freedom will just remain an idea. The power of leverage shall be your focal point in your journey towards financial freedom. Don't rely only with your two hands to make money. Rich people don't do that. They leverage their time-making-money through others. Your job is to change ways how to raise your average income to leverage income. Learn the value of your time and multiply it through others.

Invest wisely your most important asset—TIME and leverage it. If you don't practice your leverage, somebody is leveraging on your time, talent and effort. Work smart. Live a leverage life.

A great source of supplementary income

Most people are afraid of losing their jobs for security reasons. They would rather stay to a job and work for the rest of their lives instead of trying other means on how to expand their income. In this business, you can start part-time without giving up your current occupation.

Your discipline to manage your time and your commitment to take action is the key to develop your income in this venture. The more time and effort you can invest and leverage, the higher the probability to generate more supplementary cashflow to augment your immediate family needs. Don't be surprise when there will be a point in time that your supplementary income will become bigger than your primary income because somebody under your organization have a bigger dreams than yours. That's your other selves multiplying yourself.

A vehicle that can help you realize your dreams

Are you dreaming of ordinary or extra-ordinary life?

Life is how we create it. Your life is predicted and designed by your own conscious choices, not by mere chances. To experience a life of more than enough, you must also have an attitude and belief of more than enough. Networkpreneurship is a powerful vehicle that can realize your life's dreams. Don't settle for less. Live your dreams!

"Destiny is not a matter of chance, it is a matter of choice; it is not a thing to be waited for, it is a thing to be achieved." - *William Jennings Bryan*

"Until one is committed, there is hesitancy, the chance to draw back... There is one elementary truth, the ignorance of which kills countless ideas and splendid plans: That the moment one definitely commits oneself, then Providence moves too, and all the sorts of things occur to help one that would never otherwise have occurred... Whatever you can do or dream you can do, begin it. Boldness has genius, power and magic in it. Begin it now!" - Goethe

A place where you can unlock and develop your full potential

Are you appreciating or depreciating? The beauty of networkpreneurship is that you will get paid by your true value and not by the worth of your job. You can explore and develop your full capacity to express your full talent and skills in building your organization. This is a place where your mind is open to unlimited possibilities that brings out the best in people. In this business, the size of your income is equal to the size of you.

Discover your purpose in life

Networkpreneurship is all about life transformation, love and service. Doing this business properly with a strong system will lead you to building a strong relationships and selfless service to others.

Making a difference in the lives of your partners and others is your significant service to them. Guide your partners and affiliates in this business in the spirit of love.

"Nothing's without that's not within." - Goethe

Chapter III

'YOU'
FACTOR

📖 Be an Empty Cup

 During the Meiji Era (1868 1912), a Japanese Zen master welcomes in his home a university professor who wishes to dig deeper on the Zen practices and principles. The professor posed several defying questions about Zen, but the master remained silent and just served tea until it overflowed. The professor, noticing the overflowing cup and no longer restraining himself said, "How do you expect me to be convinced of Zen if you are unable to fill a cup of tea properly?" The master looked at him gently and said, "How can I show you Zen if you are like this cup, full of your own opinions and speculations?"

Learning is a minimum requirement in any successful endeavor in the business of life. You probably have the special skills and enough knowledge to help you attain your goals, but if you need to learn new ideas, free your mind first to absorb new ones better.

If you are an engineer, I shall listen as you explain to me what is best for building a house in a certain land area. If you are a surgeon, I will follow all your precautionary measures before undergoing an operation. If you are a lawyer, I will attentively listen as you cite and explain to me my rights as a citizen. All these things I would not know myself until an engineer, a surgeon, and a lawyer would enlighten me.

Individuals who get involve with the network marketing business should free his or her mind first before venturing in the business. One who aspires to become successful and highly effective in this business should be willing to undergo necessary trainings and skill-building activities to handle a solid organization of network marketing.

To learn the dynamics of this industry, you must be willing to empty your cup first to comprehend easily the principles behind network marketing taught by an upline leader. Take note that in this business, no person is smarter than the other. The first to join the business precisely has the advantage of learning first. But no worry, everybody who is willing to join can have the same opportunities as that first person. As your skills develop, you will be at par with your upline's wit and knowledge.

The good thing with the network marketing business is that it is a copy business. Remember when you are still in school and copying from a seatmate is strictly prohibited and meant a failing mark? It is not quite the same for this business. The faster you copy the system and teach others how to copy, the faster you can earn your first million.

Repetition is the mother of all learning. Learn every business detail by heart and instill it in your mind. Right attitude and appropriate skills will determine the amount of the long-term residual income you want to achieve. As Aristotle said, *"We are what we repeatedly do. Excellence, then, is not an act but a habit."*

LEARN. COMMIT. DO.

"The first problem for all of us, men and women, is not to learn but to unlearn." - Gloria Steinem

📖 Sharpen Your Saw

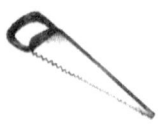

Pedro, a woodcutter, has been working for a logging company for ten years now and has never received a raise, while newcomer Florante has been with the company for only a year, and surprisingly got a raise. When Pedro asked his boss about it, the boss replied, "You are still cutting the same number of trees since we hired you, but being a results oriented company, I will be happy to give you a raise if your productivity improves." Pedro went back to work and started to hit harder and longer, but wasn't able to cut more trees. Miserably, Pedro approached Florante and asked him how he managed to cut more trees, to which Florante replied, "After cutting one tree, I take a break for five minutes and sharpen my saw."

Abraham Lincoln once said, *"If I have three hours to chop down a tree, I will spend two hours sharpening my ax."* If you stop learning, you also stop growing. When was the last time you sharpened your saw? Past success and education do not count much anymore. You must commit yourself to a lifelong learning and consistently sharpen your saw.

Practice the 5% Formula. It states that for every peso you earn, invest five centavos back to your mind for the rest of your life. This powerful concept can dramatically place you on top and will give you great success financially and in everything you will undertake.

You, yourself is your most valuable asset. Your ability to think well and act effectively depends on the quality and quantity of knowledge available for you to develop more of your potentials. You should continually upgrade your abilities to think and perform at higher levels.

In the 21st century, right information and ideas are the keys to dramatic wealth. You must develop yourself to be a highly effective person in a knowledge-worker economy. Peter Drucker said, *"The most valuable assets of the 20th century were its production equipment. The most valuable asset of a 21st century institution, whether business or non-business, will be its knowledge workers and their productivity."*

"To know and not to do is not to know." - Stephen Covey

Discover Your Genius

Each of us has a 'unique mind' that allows us to do things extremely well. Once you find that flow, your genius will automatically expose itself and in the process will reveal your true identity–your true self. The first step in knowing who you are is to find out your genius; to assess your strengths and weaknesses and to focus your 100% attention on your inherent intelligence and strength. In that level of intelligence, you can find your infinite wealth.

75

There are 7 levels of multiple intelligence according to Dr. Howard Gardner:

Verbal/Linguistic

Those who have an exceptional ability to use words, superior at explaining things–reading and writing. Able to absorb information and conceptualize details quickly. Can be a great teacher, a poet, journalist, a writer, a lawyer.

Visual/Spatial

Those who have a great ability to clearly visualize things. Superior in generating original ideas and vision. Good in using symbols and charts and can extract the meaning of it. Can clearly picture how something will look like and can easily perceive multiple dimensions. Can be an artist, a designer, a programmer, an architect.

Physical/Kinesthetic

Those who have a great ability to employ his body dynamics well learns easily by working with his hands and body motions. Can be a superior athlete, a dancer, a performer.

Musical

Those who possess a superior ability to interpret and use musical settings. Can easily remember tunes and lyrics. Employ music as a point of reference, has a natural sense of timing and rhythm, like and enjoys sounds of all type, notice and have a keen sense in the cadence of things. Can be a good singer, musician and composer.

Mathematical/Logical

Those who have an excellent ability to apply logic to systems and numerical figures. Can arrange objects logically, likes putting things in order, good at analysis, easily spots for patterns and correlation of data, calculation and planning. Can be a good accountant, mathematician, computer programmer, scientist, statistical analyst.

Introspective/Intrapersonal

Those who have a great ability to analyze his own beliefs and feelings, understand deeply his own motives and reasons for doing things, interested to daydreaming of new ideas and explore his own emotions, temperament and reflections, sharp in conceptualizing principles and concepts. Can be a good researcher, a philosopher.

Interpersonal

Those who have superior ability to relate well to other people, have empathy or diplomatic approach, can mediate arguments. Knows what to do to inter-relate with someone else, have a strong personal or public relations, likes contact with people, and sensitive to others. Can be a great leader, salesman, politician, or businessman.

"Your identity is your destiny." - Stephen Covey

Find Your Flow

What do these great achievers have in common?

Jose Rizal	Great Filipino patriot and leader
Albert Einstein	Great advocacy of mind revolution
Mother Teresa	Champion of servant leadership
Tony T. Caktiong	Business franchise expert
John Gokongwei	Business builder, billionaire
Tan Yu	Real estate builder, billionaire
Eugenio Lopez Jr.	Utility service builder, billionaire.
Brian Tracy	World class motivational speaker

John Maxwell	World class trainer on leadership
Stephen Covey	World class leadership guru
Thomas Edison	Inventor of 1093 patents
Gary Kasparov	World class chess champion
Bruce Lee	Martial Art Expert & Philosopher

They have found their "flow".

Figure 2.A

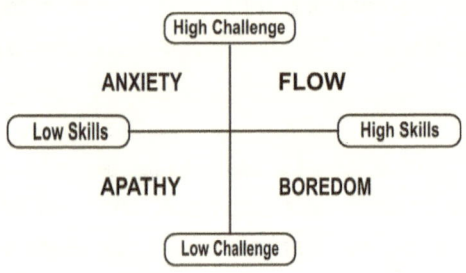

(Adapted from *Optimal Experience: Psychological studies of flow of consciousness* by Mihaly and Isabella Csikszentmihalyi)

Figure 2.A shows that if your work or job challenges are high but your skills are extremely low, you will suffer from anxiety. That happens when an average employee who cannot effectively execute his or her basic office functions because of the skill gap.

If your job challenges are low and your skills are equally low, you would experience apathy. An example is an engineer who does not even know how to plot a blueprint but does not worry a bit about losing a job because his family owns the construction business.

If your job challenges are low but your skills are extremely high, you'll get caught with boredom. That is the life for a gifted carpenter who has the skill to build big mansions and buildings but works only for a factory that produce nothing else but wooden cabinets.

If your job challenges are high and your skills are equally high, you will get the best result—*flow*. When you execute work the element of time ceases. You enjoy and love what you are doing. You feel as if you are born for the job and consider yourself as an expert.

Moreover, if you have a chance to live your life again, you would certainly choose the field of profession, where you are perfectly align to your hidden genius– your true self.

"When you are inspired by some great purpose, some extraordinary project, all your thoughts break their bounds. Your mind transcends limitations, your consciousness expands in every direction, and you find yourself in a new, great and wonderful world."

- The Yoga Sutras of Patanjali

Specialized Knowledge

If you want to be word-literate, master the art of *general knowledge*. However, if you want to be financially literate, you must master the art of *specialized knowledge* where creation of material wealth lies. Specialization, also known as *specialized lever*, is crucial in any undertaking. The better-specialized lever you develop and practice, the more financial reward you can have in life.

Category	Specialized Knowledge	Financial Reward
Employment		
Employee/ laborer	Personal hours and service	Salary/wages
Self-employment		
Doctor	Medical	Professional fee
Lawyer	Legal	Professional fee
Engineer	Construction	Professional fee

Accountant	Business/Financial	Professional fee
Programmer	Information Tech	Professional fee
Agents/Brokers	Liaison and servicing	Professional fee
Artist	Artistic	Professional fee

Business

Entrepreneur	Business building	Profit/Residual and System
Infopreneur	Information/ Idea creation	Profit/Residual
Network Marketer	Leveraging/ System duplication	Profit/Residual
Franchisor	Leveraging/ Branching	Profit/Residual
Wholesaler	Volume Selling	Profit
Retailer	Direct Selling	Profit

Investment

Stock and Bond Investor	Stock market and bond equity	Profit/Dividend
Real Estate Investor	Real state	Profit/Compound growth
Money market Investor	Money market	Profit/Compound growth
Bank depositor	Cash accumulation	Compound interest
Diverse Speculator	Risk management	Profit/Compound growth and interest

Henry Ford, founder of Ford Motors Inc., filed a libel suit against a Chicago newspaper for calling him, "ignorant man" in one of their editorials. During the court proceedings, Ford was placed in the witness stand by the prosecutors to prove to the jury the allegations that he is an ignoramus.

The prosecutors asked Henry Ford a great deal of trivial questions—from general literature, history, cultures that comprise of general knowledge that ridiculed him in court. In response to the affront questions posed to him, he bent over the stand, pointed his finger at the prosecutor and said in disgust, "If I should really want to answer the foolish question you have just asked, or any of the other questions you have been asking me, let me remind you that I have a row of electric push buttons on my desk, and by pushing the right button, I can summon to my aid men who can answer any question I desire to ask concerning the business to which I am devoting most of my efforts. Now, will you kindly tell me, why should I clutter up my mind with general knowledge, for the purpose of being able to answer questions, when I have men around me who can supply any knowledge I require?"

The famous automobile manufacturer's answer, full of truth and logic, stunned his prosecutors. The people in the courtroom realized that it was an answer not of an ignorant man but of a man of a good education.

A person is educated if he knows how to acquire his knowledge when he needs it and organize that special knowledge into a definite plan of action.

📖 Deep Down Burning Desire

 A great Indian warrior and his band of soldiers went to battle against a powerful foe, whose men outnumbered that of the warrior's. The great warrior and his men boarded their ship and sailed to the enemy's territory, and when they got to the battle area, he ordered his men to vacate the ship, unload all equipment and burn the ship that carried them. As the ship was set on fire, the great Indian warrior firmly addressed his men, "You see that ship going up in smoke, so we have no choice—we win or we perish!" They won!

Each person who wishes to succeed in everything that he or she does must be willing to burn his or her own ship and expel all sources of retreat. By doing so, one can be certain to maintain that state of mind known as the burning desire to win.

To achieve significant goals you have never achieved before, you need to start doing things you have never done before. Adapt the 'no choice' mindset. Do things as if there is no tomorrow; as if today is the last day of your life. You should want a thing so bad enough to fulfill your noble dreams and aspirations.

"You can have anything you want in life if you want it desperately enough. You must want it with an exuberance that erupts through the skin and join the energy that created the world." - *Sheila Graham*

Thomas Edison's Success Formula

Thomas Alva Edison's life is full of purpose. When he spoke of success and achievements, he would always say that the most important factors of any invention could be describe in a few words:

"They must consist of definite knowledge as to what one wishes to achieve.

One must fix one's mind on that purpose with persistence and begin searching for that which one seeks.

One must keep on searching; no matter how many times one may meet with disappointment.

One must refuse to be influence by the fact that somebody else may have tried the same idea without success.

One must keep oneself sold on the idea that the solution of the problem exist somewhere and that he will find it."

And he further said, *"The first requisite of success is the ability to apply your physical and mental energies to one problem without going weary. Genius, then, is 1% inspiration, and 99% perspiration."* He is a champion of bulldog tenacity.

"By perseverance, the snail reached the ark." - *Anonymous*

📖 Great Talent is Not Necessary

 Felipe, a man who loves to venture in any trade, wants to know the secret of success. His recent involvement in business did not prosper. His family begged him to quit dreaming and look for a good eight-to-five job.

However, Felipe did not heed their advice and instead went to see the richest man in the city. "Please, please, tell me your secret. Is it special talent? Is it intelligence?" asked Felipe.

The rich man smiled. "Let me tell you my story," the rich man began. "The first time I got involve in a business, I failed miserably. The second business I tried had failed before I even started. The third time I tried, I mismanaged. You see, I thought I needed a 50% success ratio to achieve my goals but I was proven wrong."

Felipe asked, "You mean you have to do better than 50%?"

"No, you hardly ever have to be right," answered the rich man. "I failed in all my 19 consecutive businesses. For every business, I lost almost ₱50,000 for each making it to a total of ₱950,000. Nevertheless, on my twentieth attempt, I triumphed for the first time. I may have lost ₱950,000 in my nineteen mistakes but what is that amount compared to ₱5,000,000 profit I gained, and that's only a one-shot deal."

The rich man continued, "You see! You can be wrong and fail 19 out of 20 times, but still prevail in the end. You should be persistent. You can be wrong 95% of the time but that should not keep you from trying again."

Have courage and do not quit. You only need to have one good success. When you get rich and famous, nobody will remember that you have made 19 mistakes. Why? Because your mistakes disguises themselves as your stepping-stones in achieving success.

According to study, virtually everyone starts with nothing. More than 90 percent of all financially successful people today started broke or nearly broke. The average self-made millionaire has been bankrupt or nearly bankrupt more than three times. Most wealthy people failed many times before they finally found the right opportunity that they were able to leverage into financial success.

If you never do anything, you would not commit a mistake. Get started by committing some mistakes and success will come your way. If you want to accelerate the rate of your success, you must double your rate of failure. Remember that success is on the far side of failure. Dare to fail!

"Success is 99 percent failure." - Soichiro Honda

📖 The Frog Story

 A group of frogs lived all their lives in a deep, dark, old well, and not one frog was able to jump as high as the old well's surface. One day, a tiny frog started clinging on the walls, and jumped and jumped as the others would have done, meanwhile being ridiculed by the older frogs who thought a skinny, pale frog like him should quit before he hurt himself. The skinny frog ignored their discouraging words, jumped day in and day out month after month, year after year, until one day, he made the highest jump of his life and reached the surface. As he admired the beauty of nature, the frogs left inside the well begged for his help to get out, but the little frog just hopped farther and enjoyed the beauty and abundance of the surface.

Did arrogance and vengeance fed on the tiny frog's mind, or has it not heard the pleading of his fellow amphibians? The truth is, the tiny frog is neither arrogant nor vindictive. Even from the beginning, he hears nothing of the insult and discouragement because the tiny frog is actually deaf since birth!

Most of us are easily discouraged or frustrated if someone tells us that we are not good enough to do anything. We easily give up on our dreams and ambitions to these 'dream stealers'.

Dear friend, do not let anyone take your dreams away from you. No one should stop you from fulfilling your aspirations—it is yours to fulfill! You must possess the same attitude manifested by that tiny frog. Be deaf on all disheartening criticisms. Remember that the greatest pleasure in life is to do the things that others say you cannot do.

"In life, the question is not if you will have problems, but how you are going to deal with your problems. Are you going to fail forward or to fail backward?" - John Maxwell

📖 The Value in Disaster

 It was a cold December night in West Orange, New Jersey, United States and Thomas Alva Edison's factory is in normal operation. Everybody is busy in his/her own fronts and so is the great inventor who tries to turn more of his dreams to practical realities. Edison's factory is made of steel and concrete so who could have guessed that it is not fireproofed.

On that night in 1914, a powerful blaze burst from the roof of that factory and lightened up the sky. Charles, Edison's 24-year old son, frantically searched for his father. Finally, he found the old man watching the fire; his white hair blowing in the wind and his face illuminated by the blaze.

"My heart ached for him," Charles remembers. "Here he was, 67 years old, and everything he had worked for was going up in flames. When he saw me, he shouted, 'Charles! Where's your mother?' When I told him I don't know, he said, 'Find her, bring her here! She'll never see anything like this as long as she lives'."

The next morning, Edison looked at the ruins left by the evening's fire and said this to his loss: "There's a great value in disaster. All our mistakes are burned up. Thank God, we can start anew." What a great attitude!

Thomas Alva Edison was a prolific inventor in history—holding more than 1,000 US patents in his name.

The Power of Faith

What is faith?
It is a state of mind.
The "Eternal Elixir" which gives life, power,
and action to the impulse of thought.
The only known antidote for failure.
And faith in its practical sense is the starting
point of all accumulation of riches..

- Napoleon Hill

📖 Help Yourself

 A small town experienced a flash flood and everyone was leaving for safe ground except for a man named Bartolome. He said, "God will save me. I have faith."

As the water level rose, a jeep came to rescue him but Bartolome refused, "God will save me. I have faith."

As water rose further, he went up to the second floor of his house when a boat came to help him but still he refused to go. "God will save me. I have faith," he insisted.

The water kept rising and the man climbed on to the rooftop. A rescue team in a helicopter came but he again said, "God will save me. I have faith."

Bartolome finally drowned.

When he met with the Lord, he was very disappointed. Bartolome questioned angrily, "I had complete faith in you. Why did you disregard my prayers and let me drown?"

The Lord replied, "Who do you think sent you the jeep, the boat, and the helicopter? It was I!"

📖 The Attitude Factor

Do you remember the story in the Bible of David and Goliath? Goliath was a giant man who struck fear in everyone's heart. One day, the 17-year-old shepherd David came to visit his brothers in the battlefield and asked, "Why don't you stand up and fight the giant?"

The brothers fear Goliath and spoke in unison, "Can't you see he is too big to hit?" David confidently answered, "No, he is too big to miss."

The rest is history. David killed the giant with a slingshot. Same giant, different perception.

The foundation of success is *attitude*, no more, no less. It is the most critical factor in attaining success. Our attitude determines our altitude in life and with how we treat our personal setbacks. To a positive thinker, attitude can be a stepping-stone to success; to a negative thinker, it could be an obstacle. Success, therefore, is just a matter of good or bad attitude.

"The greatest discovery of our generation is that a human being can alter his life by altering his attitudes."

- William James

📖 Doing the Unthinkable

Wilma Rudolf was born prematurely on June 23, 1940 in Tennessee, United States, and when she was four, she suffered from double pneumonia which made her left leg paralyzed, with her having to wear an iron brace. The doctors told her that she could never walk again; but her mother told her that she can do anything she wants. At age nine, Wilma took of her brace, started walking, and dreamt of becoming the greatest runner in the whole world. At age thirteen, she joined every race in her high school even if she finished last, and at the 1960 Olympic Games the impossible happened–Wilma set the world record for being the first woman ever to win three Olympic Gold medals in the same event.

Who could envision that someone who could not even walk properly be the greatest runner of her time? Wilma overcame the odds of her life to achieve her dreams and become a world champion.

You can only overcome the impossible by doing the unthinkable. Go beyond the limits!

"We must dare to think unthinkable thoughts. We must learn to explore all the options and possibilities that confront us in a complex and rapid changing world. We must dare to think about unthinkable things because when things become unthinkable, thinking stops and action become mindless." - William Fulbright

The Eagle in Storm

Did you know that an eagle knows when a storm is approaching long before it breaks?

The eagle will fly to some high spot and wait for the winds to come. When the storm hits, it sets its wings so that the wind will pick it up and lift it above the storm. While the storm rages below, the eagle is soaring above it.

The eagle does not escape the storm. It simply uses the storm to lift it higher. It rises on the winds that bring the storm. When the storms of life come upon us - and all of us will experience them - we can rise above them by setting our minds and our heart toward the greatest good.

We can allow the divine power to lift us above them to overcome the storm of life. The Divine enables us to ride the winds of the storm that bring tragedy, sickness, failure and discouragement in our lives.

Remember, it is not the burdens of life that weigh us down; it is how we handle them. We can soar above the storm of life!

"Honey bees must tap two million flowers to make one pound of honey. The sweetest rewards always come from the hardest struggles." - Anonymous

Negative Capability

Billi P.S. Lim, author of *Dare to Fail* explained that Negative Capability is the capacity to endure pain, adversities, hardships, disappointments, mistakes, and failures without being frustrated or getting pessimistic from each setback.

**Positive Thinking + Low Negative Capability =
Give up easily, full of excuses, and quitters**

**Positive Thinking + High Negative Capability =
Triumph!**

Those positive-thinking people with low negative capability or Adversity Quotient (A.Q.) will find it very hard to recover once they fall. On your journey to triumph, it is not how many times you fail but the number of times you bounces back that really matters.

The ability to handle negative situations and look beyond them positively is the key to resilience. The strength of your character will allow you to go forth, no matter how many times you fail. You will not give up. You will be able to persist.

Failing Forward

Failure is simply the price we pay to achieve success. John Maxwell stated the four rules to treat failure:

Rule # 1 There is no such thing as failures, only lessons.

Rule # 2 The lesson continues until you learn.

Rule # 3 If you do not learn the lesson, it gets harder.

Rule # 4 You will know you have learned the
lesson when you change your actions.

In life, make a habit of doing the things you fear. Doing so will certainly make your fear vanish. Learn to embrace the new definition of failure. Feel free to start moving ahead and fail forward.

"Failure is the opportunity to begin again, more intelligently." - Henry Ford

📖 The Blind and Deaf

 One bright day in Tuscumbia, Alabama, United States, Helen Keller, a girl who is totally deaf and blind, and her teacher Anne Sullivan, were drawing out water from a well pump as part of their communication exercises. Anne Sullivan was steadily pumping cool water on Helen's hand while tapping out repeatedly a five letter alphabet code on the other, and suddenly, the signals crossed Helen's consciousness with its meaning–W A T E R, that something cold flowing on her hand. Helen's teacher has succeeded in communicating with the girl Helen, who soon learned the fingertip alphabet, learned to write, master the use of Braille and the manual alphabet, and upon turning sixteen, she could speak well enough to go to preparatory school and later graduated cum laude from Radcliffe College. A truly remarkable woman, Helen Keller dedicated her life in improving the conditions of the blind and the deaf blind around the world, lecturing in more than 25 countries on the 5 major continents.

Helen Keller's ability to see the light in blindness and to hear the voice in deafness to serve others gives us a great hope and

inspiration that life is a wonderful gift from God that should be cherish and enjoy for a grand purpose.

"The most pathetic person in the world is someone who has sight, but has no vision." - Helen Keller

"There is no chance, no destiny, no fate, can circumvent or hinder or control the firm resolve of a determined soul. Gifts count for nothing, will alone is great." - Ella Wheeler Wilcox

📖 The Strong Seed

Once upon a time, a seed was blown by a strong wind into a crevice of a rock. Though imprisoned in the dark hole, the seed never surrendered to its misfortune. Determined to survive, it absorbed the moisture of the morning dew until its tiny root hairs sprouted, giving it more nutrients to grow up. One sunny morning, a little leaf popped out from the seed, smiled at the sun, laughed at the rain, waved with the wind and proudly exclaimed, "I have overcome!"

Like that strong seed, each one of us has that same power within our hearts to serve our own purpose of surmounting all the odds that shall come our way. To be able to bounce back after every fall; to be able to break free from any limitations; and to claim our rightful place in this planet–to be the master of our own circumstances and the creator of our own destiny.

"Man is not the creature of circumstances. Circumstances are the creatures of man." - Benjamin Disraeli

Persistency Test

Persistence is to man's character as carbon is to steel. Persistency is that one indispensable character that must go hand-in-hand with your pursuit to success. Resolve in your subconscious mind that you must never give up, no matter what happens in any of your dealings.

The courage to persist all adversities in life is one quality that can guarantee the achievement of your life's goals. Your ability to persist longer than anyone else will be your greatest personal asset; it is the true measure of your character and your ability to succeed.

Do not forget that life is a series of unending trials. To enjoy the grandeur of life, you should be able to pass the persistency test. You may not know it, but you take this test whenever you are confronted by all sorts of difficulties and crisis in life. This is the right time to show your true self and reveal to everyone what you are truly made of.

If you get past this test as the strong seed has, you will be like a force of nature–unstoppable and unrelenting. You will be that person who never gives up and carries on no matter how tough are the setbacks. You will keep on finding a way—to go over it, under it, around it or through it.

"Nothing can take the place of persistence. Talent will not; nothing is more common than unsuccessful men with talent. Genius will not; unrewarded genius is almost a proverb. Education will not; the world is full of educated derelicts. Persistence and determination alone are omnipotent." - Calvin Coolidge

📖 The Lost Fortune

 A man enchanted by the gold rush went to Colorado to excavate until he discovered the source of gold, covered it, and went home to buy a quarry machine. He came back with his friends and relatives and started quarrying again but the vein of the gold ore was gone and the pot of gold was no longer there. They drilled on until they got exhausted by frustration, decided to quit and sold the quarry machine to a junk shop owner. The junk shop owner then

consulted a mining engineer and found the vein of the ore and the pot of gold just three feet away from where the first owner had stopped drilling.

One of the most common causes of failure in life is the habit of quitting when one experiences a temporary defeat. You must possess the willpower to keep going on until you accomplish your aspirations in life. Quit quitting.

"Never, never, never, never give up." - Winston Churchill

📖 The Rock

 Once a great king placed a big rock on a road and hid behind the bushes to see if anyone would try to remove the rock. A great reward awaits the person who has the right virtue, he thought. Many people passed by and ignored the big rock until a peasant labored to remove it and found a purse lying on that same place where the rock had been. The purse contains several gold coins and a note from the king saying that the gold coins shall belong to the person who can remove the big rock out of this road.

Opportunities oftentimes disguise themselves as adversities. It may be concealed in every problem you may encounter. Search the good seed in every adversity that will come your way and it may benefit you a rewarding opportunity. Open up to a new range of possibilities, unveil the mysteries and keep up with its adventures. Treat each problem as an opportunity for a greater benefit. If you are prepared to meet the odds, the solution will appear in just a snap.

Remember that in every problem, obstacle, heartache, and misfortune contains with it the "seed" of equal or greater benefits.

"The heights by great men reached & kept were not attained by a sudden flight, but they, while their companion slept, were toiling upward in the night." - W. Longfellow

📖 The Story of Harland Sanders

 One day, an old man realized he wanted to do something before his days are over, and made a list of a hundred possible ventures to engage in. With his mother's chicken recipe standing out, he kept on improving his mother's recipe and started making batches of chicken, travelling by car, in 1952, from one restaurant to another across the country, to search for somebody who can support him financially. After 1009 failed attempts, somebody finally agreed to his chicken recipe, and in 1964 at age 74, Harland Sanders had more than 600 franchise outlets for his chicken product in the United States and Canada. A quick service restaurant pioneer, he has become a symbol of entrepreneurial spirit.

As of year-end 2013, Harland Sanders has reached more than 18,000 franchise restaurants in more than 100 countries and territories around the world.

Probably, you have been eating in one of its food outlets. The name of this fast-food restaurant is Kentucky Fried Chicken or KFC, as popularly known. It all began when an old man risked his $105 Social Security check to start a business at a glorious age of 65.

If Mr. Harland Sanders made it, why cannot we?

"Remember that all who succeeds in life get off to a bad start, and pass through many heartbreaking struggles before they arrived. The turning point in the lives of those who succeed usually comes at the moment of some crisis through which they are introduced to their other selves." - Napoleon Hill

"Gold is tested by fire, and human character is tested in the furnace of humiliation. Trust the Lord and He will help you." - Sirach

Chapter IV

PRINCIPLES
OF
PROSPECTING

Prospecting

Prospecting means to explore or find something of great value (for example: gold, silver, diamond, oil, money, people, etc.).

The 3 Laws of Fishermen
Go where the fishes are

Fishermen go where the fishes are—in the ocean. In the network marketing business, fishes are everywhere! All you have to do is learn the three crucial skills for this system.

The first crucial skill is to *see more people*. Talk to anyone who will stand still long enough to listen to you. The second is to *see more people*. Keep calling people. You may be the best presenter in town but if you do not search for more prospects, you will be out of the business. You can be an excellent dresser and have a great personality, but without significant volume of presentation, you will only be an average.

The third and the last crucial skill is to *see more people*. Many networkpreneurs just go along with the business and never reach their potential. They think it is because they were not able to convince their prospects but it is quite the opposite, they were not able to come across with the right prospects. That is a big difference so talk to anyone and go where the fishes are.

Do not ever get tired to tell your story. Your residual income is in direct proportion to the number of people that you can enroll in your organization and become your business builders. Start with your *warm list* of prospects (family members, friends, associates and other close relatives) before you try the *cold list* or strangers.

As the saying goes, "The grass looks greener on the other side of the fence." That is where your prospects are. You should offer this opportunity as a special gift to someone.

Use the right bait

The fishermen use the right bait to catch the right fish. In a network marketing business, you must have the right attitude, skills and the tools to motivate and guide your prospects for the business. The quality of your trainings and support system will determine the level of commitment, bonding and growth you establish with your business partners. The cardinal rule in building a solid and effective network organization is to:

Help them first—your partners and associates—to get what they want in life before you get what you want. We should use the business to make great people and not to use people to make great business.

Practice the principle of giving: If you want joy, give joy to others; if you want love, learn to give love; if you want material affluence, help others become materially affluent, too. The more you give the more you will receive and abundance will evolve in your life. Remember that anything of value in life only multiplies when it is sincerely given.

If you want all the good things in life, learn to share to everyone the good things in life. Reciprocation is the dynamics of seed-giving. You will receive in proportion to what you have planted and a reward insured by the Principle of the Harvest.

Sincere giving is like planting seeds in God's garden. God nurtures them, multiplies them and makes them fruitful. God brings forth an abundant harvest. God, Himself being the gardener, will see to it that you will yield a bountiful harvest. Let the virtue of giving come from a pure heart. For the heart, not the gift makes a sincere giver.

"No man becomes rich unless he enriches others."

- Andrew Carnegie

Keep on fishing

The fishermen drop their nets at the right spots as many as they could to catch more fishes. They practice the principle of average. The Principle of Average states that:

If you do something the same way over and over again, under the same condition or circumstance, you will get a constant set of results.

If the goal is to catch 1000 kilos and they catch an average of 50 kilos per drop of net; they need to drop the nets in the water by 20 times in order to achieve the desired harvest of one thousand kilos. It is through *increase activity* that you can achieve your desired result.

In network marketing business, you can also apply the principle of average. This is a number's game business and *new blood* is the lifeblood of this industry. You have to look for desire, not need!

If you understand the principle of average, you will never entertain any failures, discouragements, and obstacles that may cross your way. Establish your own average and improve it. It is the name of the game.

"The cattle breeder says, 'In order to have more milk, find more cows'." - Anonymous

The Law of the Harvest

All abundance in life lies in the law of the harvest. A person who desires to get his or her share of the 'wealth of life' should follow this simple but profound law of the farmers, which is also the governing law of life.

As to farming, the farm soil is first prepared and well sorted before planting at the right season. The role of a good farmer is not just to plant seeds but also to make sure that they plant good seeds. He believes that spoiled seeds will produce bad harvest and good seeds will promise a thousand forests.

Next, the farmer must diligently attend to the cultivation—from watering, weeding, giving the right amount of fertilizer and finally to protect it from bad weather.

After a long wait, a good harvest will follow. Eliminating any of these natural processes will risk a fruitful harvest.

This is also true if we desire for success in life. You should have a definite goal and a specific plan of action. Plant your wealth seed—your God given potential—with quality time and effort in your own farm. Do all the necessary process by providing more and better service to your concerns, by virtue of courage, perseverance, and commitment to grow.

After the cultivation process, you should be willing to prolong your patience and keep the faith that your plant will have ample fruits in due time. That is the law of the harvest. If you abide by this natural flow, assure yourself of earning the bountiful harvest of life.

This law is also known as the law of cause and effect or Karma, which is the iron law of human destiny. It states that there is a specific effect for every cause; for every action, there is an equal reaction. It further reiterates that success in life is not an accident.

Mother Nature unfolds this inevitable law. All lasting results are produced in a sequence and are governed by this law. Financial and life success is the result of doing certain things or actions repeatedly until you achieve the fruits of financial and time freedom you desire.

The law of the harvest also advocates that if you follow the footsteps of real successful people, you will eventually attain the results that these successful people have achieved in their lives. What you sow is what you reap.

"There is a wonderful mystical law of nature that the three things we crave most in life—happiness, freedom, and peace of mind are attained by giving them to someone else." - Lawrence Stern

Master Prospector

 Assume that you are a professional pearl hunter and for every hour, I give you a bucket of 100 oysters each. Among those oysters, only 2 have pearls inside and the other 98 are all empty.

You take one oyster cut it open and found that one oyster is empty. So you carefully put the shells back together, hold it between your hands to keep it warm and wait for a day for the oyster to conceive a pearl. As a professional, would you do this?

Of course, you would not! You would throw the empty oyster away and reach for another until you found one with a pearl, right? This is how the master prospector finds his valuables.

"New blood is the lifeblood of Network Marketing business." - *Anonymous*

Where are Your Aces?

 Do you play card games? Did you notice that in most card games the aces are the most valuable among a deck of 52 cards? Those are your winning cards and are limited to only 4. If you randomly pick one card at a time from a deck, you must draw a card after another until you get an ace.

If you are fortunate enough, you might find your aces in the 2nd, 5th, 8th, or 10th. However, if you are already in the 35th or the 45th pick but still no ace appears, would you quit drawing? Certainly not, you will continue to draw the card until you get your winning aces.

In network marketing, the master prospector's role to convince people to join the business is only secondary. The primary role would be to explore or to sort through people who are willing to venture into the system. The master prospector must continuously draw from a deck of cards until he or she finds the aces and must not be discouraged by a negative turnout.

If you really want to be an effective prospector, just keep on doing your task and offer the system to as many individuals as you can. If you have already introduced the system to, for instance, 48 prospects and not one has yet to respond to the opportunity, it is not the right time to quit. Instead, rejoice! Just carry on drawing a card after another. Your valuable aces or business builders may be just one card away.

"The best way to find your self is to lose yourself in the service of others." - Mahatma Gandhi

📖 Parable of Ham and Egg

 Do you know where your delicious Ham and Egg come from, long before it is brought in the breakfast table? For the egg, a hen only has to lay a number of eggs, but for the ham, it is a different story. Before you can produce the delicious ham, you need the cooperation of the pig. Unlike the hen, the pig does not simply involve itself, but it commits and sacrifices itself to produce the ham.

In relation to the network marketing business, if you really want to have a lasting success, involvement is not enough. You must commit yourself and sacrifice your conveniences to attain your worthy goals in life.

"If you want to start your own business, you should possess certain qualities like integrity, honesty, thrift, diligence, and a willingness to take measured risks. It's 'hard work' really. You cannot just build a business on dreams." - John Gokongwei

📖 The Restaurant Story

A sponsor discusses to his prospect how to start a network marketing business.

Sponsor: Do you know anything about running a restaurant?

Prospect: No.

Sponsor: Let's say you wanted to open your own restaurant and wanted to do it slowly. You aren't sure you can handle it so you decided to open only once a week. You don't want to take big risks so you will open only for two hours during Friday evenings.

Prospect: I feel comfortable with that.

Sponsor: To make things easier, you should arrange for customers to come by invitation only. You don't want too many guests on your first night. I will help you for the first couple of Fridays.

Prospect: So far, this sounds easy enough.

Sponsor: We'll invite only four of your friends on the opening night. You and I will serve their meals. If they like the food, we'll ask them to pass the word to others.

Prospect: Sounds fair.

Sponsor: On the second Friday night, we will tell each of your friends to bring one new guest. Now that will make eight customers. Our experience from our first night must improve our service for the succeeding Friday evenings.

Prospect: Sure. Eight people wouldn't be any problem for the two of us.

Sponsor: On the third Friday night, we will again ask each of our eight customers to come along with another friend. Now we have sixteen guests to serve. We still plan to open only two hours once a week and keep this business part-time. Maybe we'll extend hours to another weeknight. We don't want more than 16 guests at a time.

Prospect: That makes sense.

Sponsor: Let's open and serve on Tuesday nights. We'll hire a qualified assistant from our set of customers and train him or her to adapt our work and start the first Tuesday with a bang. Our Friday nights will still be easy to operate and we'll send some of our customers to Tuesday evenings.

Prospect: I think I get the picture. Maybe Network Marketing won't be so hard if I take one step at a time. Sign me up. I'll invite four of my friends for a Friday night opportunity meeting.

Anyone especially you can easily learn the network marketing business if you execute your plans in accordance with your goal one-step at a time. Your upline partner would be much willing to guide and help you in your newly found business. You can create a T.E.A.M. (Together Everyone Accomplish More) and a S.Y.S.T.E.M. (Save Your Self Time, Energy, Money). Both of you becomes an unlimited synergy. In network marketing, 1 + 1 is not = 2; it is = 11!

The 5-Step Empowerment
Dr. John Maxwell suggested a 5-step empowerment principle:

I DO IT   I Model
I DO IT AND YOU WATCH   I Mentor

YOU DO IT AND I WATCH	I Monitor
YOU DO IT	You Move Forward
YOU DO IT WITH SOMEBODY ELSE	We Multiply

This principle is an effective system in developing the potential skills of other people who works side by side with an apprentice until the latter masters his or her own craft and be able to pass it on to others.

People becomes more productive if nurtured. We can empower them by giving the B.E.S.T. (Believe in them; Encourage them; Share with them; and Trust them). Step-by-step, we can do it!

"Each of us is an idea of the Great Gull, an unlimited idea of freedom. Your whole body, from wingtip to wingtip is nothing more than your thought itself, in a form you can see. Break the chains of your thought, and you break the chains of your body, too...We are free to go where we wish and to be what we are." - Jonathan Livingston Seagull

Flying 'V'

 It is during fall when you see a flock of geese flying along in a V formation heading south for the winter. You might ask how they do it and consider what science has discovered. As each bird flaps its wings, it creates uplift for the bird behind another. By flying in a 'V' formation, the whole flock adds at least 71% greater flying range than a bird flying on its own.

People who share a common sense of direction and community can reach their target quick and easy if they are bounded by one thrust. When a goose falls out of the formation, it feels the drag and quickly returns to its original position to maximize the lifting power of the bird in front. If we have as much sense as a goose, we will stay in alignment with those who are heading the same way as we are.

It creates a dynamic synergy and co-operation among the members that pushes and bonds the group to keep them going.

"I can do what you can't do, and you can do what I can't do; together we can do great things." - Mother Teresa

Taproot Principle

 From a single acorn, a great oak grows! Feeding a giant oak tree means literally feeding hundreds of miles of roots under the ground. Among these roots is a taproot digging deeper into the soil than the other roots. Its purpose is to tap water from its source to sustain the life of a tree during a dry spell.

In network marketing, your vital role when you sponsor a new associate is to develop a "taproot" level in that associate's downline organization to sustain you a continuous flow of residual income even in times of drought. This is also regarded as the tapping of the critical mass—the reservoir of your residual income.

"You won't harvest big unless you plant well." - Josiah Go

Chapter V

GOAL SETTING
AND TIME
MANAGEMENT

Goal Setting

The members of Class '53 of Yale University were collectively interviewed if they had put Into writing their plans and goals. Only three percent has actually done so and in 1973, or twenty years later, the results were surprising. Researchers discovered in a follow-up interview that among the surviving members of that class, the three percent who had set specific goals and had a written plan of action for achieving those goals had amassed a financial wealth greater than the rest or 97% of the class combined.

Have specific written goals and execute it with 100% commitment and perseverance.

"A goal is a dream with a deadline." - Napoleon Hill

"Until you commit your goals to paper, your intentions are like seeds without a soil." - Anonymous

Set Your Goal

The Andrew Carnegie's goal setting principle:

The starting point of all great achievements in life is Burning Desire. The method, by which desire for riches can be transmuted into its financial equivalent, consists of 6 definite, practical steps:

1. Fix in your mind the exact amount of money you desire. It is not sufficient merely to say "I want plenty of money." Be definite as to amount. There is a psychological reason for definiteness in value.

2. Determine exactly what you intend to give in return for the money you desire. There is no such reality as something for nothing.

3. Establish a definite date when you intend to possess the money you desire.

4. Create a definite plan for carrying out your desire, and begin at once, whether you are ready or not, to put this plan into action.

5. *Write out a clear, concise statement of the amount of money you intend to acquire, name the time limit for its acquisition, state what you intend to give in return for the money, and describe clearly the plan through which you intend to accumulate it.*

6. *Read your written statement aloud, twice daily, once before retiring at night, and once after arising in the morning.*

If you truly desire money that it becomes an obsession, you will have no difficulty in convincing yourself that you will acquire it. The objective is to want money and be determined to have it.

In reality, the manifestation of our desire is twice apparent. The first is manifested in the mind–the *blueprint*, and the second is *physical*–the final product. Take the construction of a home, for instance. You have to make a draft first before installing a nail into its place. You have to visualize the kind of house you want to build and work with ideas. Then you reduce it to a blueprint and develop construction plans. All of these must be done before the earth is touched. If estimations has not been done, you may incur expensive costs for major changes for the renovations of the same house, which is the physical creation itself.

Similarly, if you want to create a solid source of income, you should clearly define what you are trying to accomplish. Be definite as to the amount of money you want to create. Determine also what you intend to give in return for the money you desire. Write a definite plan of action and set a deadline for accomplishing it. Begin with the end in mind.

"In the long run men hit only what they aim at."

- Henry David Thoreau

📖 Focus Your Desire, Desire Your Focus

A student of Socrates once asked the Greek philosopher what he should do to become enlightened. The philosopher shoved his student into the river and submerged him until he was close to drowning and asked, "What are you thinking while I hold you under the water?" The student answered, "When there is no sign that you would release me, all I could think of is: air! air! Give me air!" Socrates smiling and said, "When you desire enlightenment with the same intensity, you will soon have it."

The same applies to achieving your goals. You must desire it wholeheartedly. Desire is the fuel that propels you to influence your thoughts and actions to attain your objectives. Burning desire helps you overcome obstacles and draws inspiration from your subconscious mind.

A strong desire together with proactive beliefs, a keen intention and continuous action will attract you to people, circumstances and situations necessary for you to become successful. The moment you make a decision to fulfill your goals, the whole universe conspires to make it happen.

"Anybody can wish for riches, and most people do, but only a few know that a definite plan, plus a burning desire for wealth, are the only dependable means of accumulating wealth." - Napoleon Hill

The Test of Life and Death

Let us say you already have your own family and a happy one. Unfortunately, the wheel of life jammed and your only son was diagnosed with a lung cancer. The doctor said he only has a month to live if not attended at once. You are stuck in the middle of nowhere and you do not know what to do.

Your son's illness can be cured and he would only be saved if you strictly follow the doctor's prescription which says that you have to produce an amount of ₱200,000 in a matter of one week to avail the necessary medication. It is rather odd, but the prescription says that the money must not come from your family's own resources but from other people who can give or lend you a sum of not higher than ₱1,000 for each. Moreover, that prescription starts today.

What will you do? Definitely, you will immediately start to find the needed sum of money from more than one hundred persons as prescribed to save the life of your only son. You will do it no matter what it takes!

In a similar view, the only choice you have if you want to become a successful and effective networkpreneur is for you to commit your goals and achieve it for yourself and for your loved ones no matter what it takes. Remember, the greatest risk in life is to risk nothing.

Acid Test
DOUBT = NO ACTION = NO RESULT
BELIEF = ACTION = RESULT

Proactive belief system is the acid test in transforming your life goals to reality.

If you are in doubt, there will be no action and apparently will not generate a positive result.

Nevertheless, if you have a strong belief, action will follow and will reward you with a favorable result!

"Concentration is the secret of strength in politics, in war, in trade, in short in all management of human affairs." - Ralph Waldo Emerson

Goal Achievement
Answer the following focal questions to assess your ability to create and achieve your present and future financial fortress:

How much do you want to earn this year? Why?
How much do you want to earn next year? Why?

How much do you want to earn per month five
> (5) years from today? Why?

How much do you want to be worth when you retire?

What is your exit strategy?

What is your plan of action to earn/acquire
> this amount of money?

What actions will you do every month, every week,
> and everyday to achieve your financial goal?

If you believe you cannot fail, what one thing
> would you dare to do with your life? Why?

The starting point of any *goal setting* and *goal achievement* is based on the intensity of your desire to achieve your goal and the degree of your commitment and discipline to take focus actions until you accomplish it.

Brian Tracy, one of the most effective and expert trainer in the field of personal development, business growth, strategic marketing and management, and leadership who coaches millions of people revealed the power of goal and the 7-steps on how to set and achieve any goals in life—financial, mental, emotional and spiritual.

Follow these proven 7 focal-step formula on goal setting and goal achievement and live a life of abundance:

1. *Decide exactly what you want.* Be clear and specific in each area of your life. Clarity and definiteness of purpose is the key in achieving your goal. Decide on it!

2. *Write it down clearly and specifically.* Make it measurable. Only 3% of adults have written goals and everyone else works for them. Here's an example: To increase my present income by 50% in the next 6 months. A goal that is not in writing is merely a fantasy. It has no energy behind it. Write it!

3. Set a deadline for your goal and, if it is a big goal, set sub-deadlines. Your subconscious mind thrives on time-specific goals. It uses a deadline as a forcing system to bring your 24 hours a day once you have programmed it into your subconscious mind. Set a deadline!

4. Make a list of everything you will have to do to achieve your goal. Add to your list as you think of new tasks and activities. Keep adding to your list until it is complete. Make a list!

5. Organize your list into a plan of action. Decide what you need to do first and what you need to do later. Apply the 20/80 rule. Decide what must be done and in what order. Organize your list of priority by determining which task is more important and which activities are less important. Organize it!

6. Take action on your plan immediately. Do something, do anything, get started. Many people fail because they don't take action on their goals and plan. Take the first step and put the entire goal achieving process into action. Act now!

7. Resolve to do something everyday that moves you toward your major goal, whatever it is at the moment. This step is very important. This discipline of doing something everyday enables you to develop and maintain *momentum*. Daily action increases your determination and gives you vitality. This single resolution, daily action moves you faster and faster towards your goal, and moves your goal faster and faster towards you. Do something everyday!

Just remember, whatever you think, feel and believe, and take committed actions, you can attain it. Nobody can stop you from achieving your goals in life if you wills it!

Time Bank

What if you have open a bank which credits your account each morning with ₱86,400 but its remaining balance is not retroactive for each succeeding day. Furthermore, no cash could be retained in your account. Each evening, the bank cancels whatever part of the amount you had failed to use during the day. Most probably, you would withdraw every centavo deposited in this bank.

Well, you do have such a bank and its name is TIME. Every morning it credits you 86,400 seconds. Each night it rules off whatever seconds you have failed to utilize for a good purpose. This account carries over no balances and allows no overdrafts. If you fail to use the day's deposits, the loss is yours, as there are no withdrawals for tomorrow.

Put value on your time, just as you do with your money. Every single second of your life must be invested in productive and noble activities. Time is wealth.

"Know the true value of time; snatch, and enjoy every moment of it. No idleness, no laziness, and no procrastination: never put off till tomorrow what you can do today." - Lord Chesterfield

The 2-Step Time Management

Step 1: Identify what is important

📖 Empty Jar

A time management expert placed a jar on the table and placed a dozen rocks inside until it is filled to the top and asked his class, "Is the jar full?" and everyone said, "Yes." He then pulled out a bucket of gravel and dumped some in the jar, followed by a good amount of sand and a pitcher of water until the jar could no longer hold any more. And every time he adds something inside the jar he asked the students if the jar is full. Then he said, "What is exhibited in front of the class points out that: If you don't put the big rocks first, you'll never get them in at all!"

What are the big rocks or goals in your life? How much important is it to you? When do you want to accomplish it? Whatever it is, you must put emphasize and focus on your most significant goals and purpose in life. Just make sure that everything is in balance. Remember to put these goals in your priorities, or you would not be able to fit them at all in your life. Put first things first.

Step 2: Choosing Blue Chip activity

Some activities bring us satisfaction or take us closer to our goals and objectives. Others are simply overhead—things that have to get done but do not contribute much to our progress. One of the most powerful time management skills is the ability to identify the difference between satisfaction and overhead. To evaluate the activities of our lives, we can put them into chip categories as follows:

Blue Chip: High payoff that can lead directly to your priorities.

Red Chip: Important activity that contribute to the accomplishment of your goals that can be done by someone else.

White Chip: Activity that consumes time with a little payoff. This time robber may seem urgent; it has little to do with your priorities and should be eliminated from your daily routine.

The biggest loss of effectiveness may be derived from focusing not on our priorities instead of choosing the activities and behaviors that will have the biggest return. We are creatures of habit and often do what lies in front of us, the white chips rather than look for the blue chips activities.

Here is an easy formula for identifying your priorities:

Blue Chip	**- Do it!**
Red Chip	**- Delegate it!**
White Chip	**- Ignore it!**

The 2 areas of Blue Chips activities:

Planning

The difference between average players and high achievers is the amount of time they spend on highly productive activities or the Blue Chip. The primary tool for blue chips activities is to have a *to do list*, prioritize the tasks and follow the plan. While urgent situations may require a change of plan may occur, it should be an exception rather than a rule.

Focus and Awareness

Frequently ask yourself this question: "Will this Blue Chip activity allow me to realize my objectives?" When others say that they practice blue chips activities, everyone else understands that their commitment, focus and ability must not to be distracted by lesser important tasks. To help remind yourself of the importance of this concept, you may need to carry a blue chips card with you or place it on your desk where you can see it all the time. At the end of each day, review your activities. Did you spend enough time on your Blue Chips? Did you ignore the time robbing White Chips? Have you effectively used your time by delegating the Red Chips to others?

Many time-robbing activities are simply bad habits. Your Blue Chips can help you break unproductive habits, which will keep you from attaining your significant goals and objectives.

(Adapted from *Leadership, Teambuilding, and culture change* by Senn-Delaney Leadership Consulting Group.)

"The ability to concentrate and to use time well is everything." - Lee Iacocca

"I am personally persuaded that the essence of the best thinking in the area of goal setting and time management can be captured in a single phrase: Organize and Execute around Priorities." - Stephen Covey

The 20/80 Rule

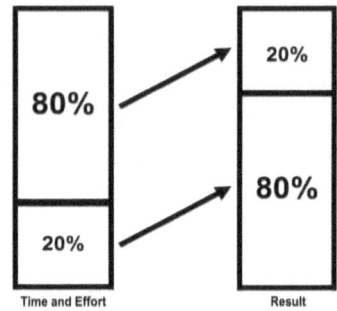

In 1906, Italian economist Vilfredo Pareto created a mathematical formula to represent the unequal distribution of wealth in his country. He observed that 20% of the people owned 80% of the nation's wealth.

In the late 1940's, Dr. Joseph Juran conducted a similar study and proves the same assessment. He acknowledged this principle and later called it the "vital few and trivial many" which states that 20% of something are responsible for 80% of its results. The 20/80 Rule, also known as the Pareto principle, states that in anything, the few (20 per centum) is vital and the many (80 per centum) are trivial.

In Pareto's case, it means that 20% of the people own 80% of the wealth. In Dr. Juran's studies, he qualifies that 20% of the defects causes 80% of the problems. Project managers know that 20% of the work (the first 10% and the last 10%) consume 80% of the time and resources. You can apply the 20/80 Rule to almost anything, from the science of management to the physical world.

Time and Effort

20% of our time and effort produces 80% of the results.

Investment

20% of our investment earned 80% of our passive income.

Products

20% of the products bring in 80% of the profit.

Business Organization

20% of the people will make 80% of business success.

Belief

20% of our belief system will determine 80% of our fate.

Leadership

20% of the people influence 80% of followers.

Work

20% of our work provides us 80% of our satisfaction.

Spirituality

20% of our faith gives us 80% meaning of our life.

Pareto's principle reminds you to focus on the 20% that greatly matters of all the things you do during the day. Those 20% produce 80% of your results. Identify and focus on those things. When the itineraries of the day begin to drain your time, remind yourself of the 20% you need to focus on. If something is not going to get done, make sure it is not part of your major priorities.

Do not just work smart, work smart on the right things. Plan your work and work your plan!

"Wisdom is the power to put our time and our knowledge to the proper use." - *Thomas Watson*

The Principle of Increasing Returns

The principle of increasing returns states that the more you focus on doing the few things that represent the most valuable use of your time, the better you can administer your activities will take you a lesser time to accomplish each one.

The return on your effort and energy will greatly increase. This principle further explains that life is a study of attention. Where your attention goes, your heart goes also. Your ability to divert your attention from an activity of lower value to an activity of a higher value is essential to everything you accomplish in life. Any objective or things you focus single-mindedly on could significantly improves your present life condition.

7 Skills to Higher Productivity

Find your flow. Do things you are better at.

Focus on Blue Chips. Work on higher-value activities.

Work harder in all things that you do.

Work faster.

Work longer hours.

Cluster your tasks or multi-task.

Simplify your work.

"The best way to predict the future is to create it."

- Peter Drucker

Be Here Now!

Now is the only time that really matters. Past is past and you cannot do anything to change it. The past is history, the future is a mystery and this moment is a gift. The point of your power and control is in the present. The choices you would make right now will shape your destiny. You can design your life the way you want it to be. Be 100% present at this moment. The future is right here—today.

"The future—something which everyone reaches at the rate of sixty minutes an hour, whatever he does, wherever he is." - C.S. Lewis

"Time is the currency of the 21st century." - Brian Tracy

Chapter VI

CODES
OF
LEADERSHIP

The True Leader

Leadership is the ability to convey to people their personal worth and potential; it is the virtual process of modeling, path finding, aligning, and empowering people to find and express their true nature and share it for the common good of all.

According to James Hunter, *"Leadership begins with the will, the unique ability of human beings to align our intentions with our actions and behavior. With a good will, we can choose to love (the verb), which is about identifying and meeting the legitimate needs, not wants, of those we lead. When we meet the needs of others, we will, by definition, be called upon to serve or even sacrifice. When we serve and sacrifice for others, we established Authority or Influence like the law of harvest. When we have already built authority or influence on other people, then we have earned the right to be called a leader."*

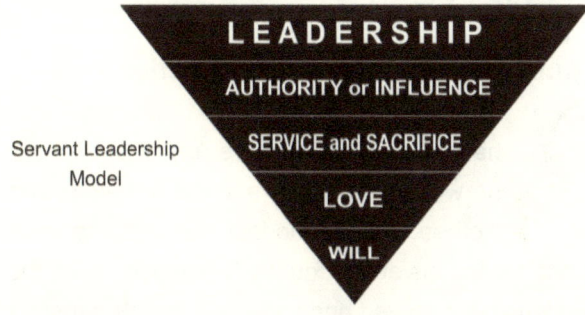

Servant Leadership Model

"True leadership is built upon Moral Authority or Influence, which built upon Service and Sacrifice, which is built upon Love. When you lead with authority, you will, by definition, be called upon to extend yourself, love, service, and even sacrifice for others. The role of true leader is to serve and the greatest leader is the one who served the most." - James Hunter

The servant-leadership model is shown in the *Bible* through a shepherd. The flock is not there for the sake of the shepherd; the shepherd is there for the sake of the flock. The rise and fall of every institution, organization or business is fundamentally attributed to leadership.

The following personas advocate and practice the principle of servant-leadership model: Jesus Christ, Joan of Arc, Mahatma Gandhi, Mother Teresa of Calcutta, Martin Luther King, Princes Diana, Dr. Jose Rizal, and Benigno Aquino Jr.

They are true leaders and true servants in their own right. Their unconditional service to others is the pathway to their real significance as a person. Have a servant's heart—the heart of a true leader.

"People don't care how much you know, until they know how much you care." - John Maxwell

Influence: The Voice of a True Leader

Mohandas Gandhi (1869-1948) was not a ruler of nations, nor did he have any scientific gifts. He had no wealth, no home and did not even own a suit of clothes. Yet this modest man did what others before him did not. He led his entire country to freedom using the principle of non-violence. He served and sacrificed for this cause until it bore the fruit of independence.

In history, majority of the world's national heroes are warriors, but Gandhi ended British rule over his native India without striking a single blow. A frail man, he devoted his life to peace and unity in order to achieve social and political progress. Gandhi was one of the gentlest of men and a devoted patriot. He had an iron core of determination and nothing could change his convictions.

He came by power by inducing over two hundred million people to coordinate, mind and body, in spirit of harmony for a definite purpose–freedom through non-violence.

In short, Gandhi accomplished a miracle, for it is a miracle when he influenced the minds of millions of people not by force or coercion but through unity in spirit of faith and love, and achieve this astounding feat. His good traits gained him a tremendous voice of influence that led to India's independence. Some observers call him a master politician. Others believe him to be a saint. To millions of Hindus, he was their beloved Mahatma, meaning the 'great soul'.

"Leadership is the ability or skill of influencing people to work enthusiastically towards goals identified as being for the common good, with character that inspires confidence. It should not be based on Force or Power but on 'Authority or Influence'." - James Hunter

"Leaders see the way... Leaders see the connections... Leaders see others... Leaders see within... Answers belong to the eyes that see them." - Stephen Covey

"The vision that you glorify in your mind, the ideal that you enthrones in your heart—this you will build your life by; this you will become." - James Allen

The Network General

If you are an army general and you send a platoon of 1,000 soldiers out on the frontlines of the battlefield of which there are no capable sergeants, lieutenants, and a captain, what do you think will happen when the firings begin?

Chaos, right? If there is no organization and no leadership, your 1,000 troop members will prove to be very ineffective. Some will hide and others may desert the platoon. Some might even give up or surrender. In the absence of leadership, a group of people, even highly productive ones, will be in for a lost command.

In network marketing, some leaders also fail to organize their own network of associates to get the business going, just like that army general.

Presuming that you are a proficient general and you are sending your platoon of 1,000 soldiers on the frontlines with 5 sergeants, 2 lieutenants and 1 captain all effective in their line of duty. This second platoon has leadership and is more likely to hold its position, work together and be very effective in their combat to fulfill the mission.

The difference? 8 good leaders. Just as the army general who delegates authority to his junior officers to lead and motivate his troops, a highly productive network leader must also be like one.

Wide-scale network marketing organizations are not superheroes that can sponsor a thousand associates; they are professional prospectors who can sponsor a few good associates and help each of them to get 100-200 associates to join their organization.

Your role as an effective network leader is to set up and delegate a chain of counselors or leaders that can influence and support your associates in achieving their goals. Leadership is all about bringing out the best in people. It is the cornerstone of building an effective and solid organization of network marketing.

"It is crucial to our future that we find ways to lead better. Because in the final analysis, it's not the general who wins, but the army. And the more that you can help people be self-sufficient, proud of themselves, and truly skillful, the more the organization is going to accomplish."

- Ruben Mark

"When the general is weak and lacks discipline, when training and instructions are not clear, when the duties of officers and men are not distinct, and when the formation is slovenly, the result is utter disorganization." - Sun Tzu

"True leaders are those who lead by serving others. Potential followers will freely respond only to individuals who are chosen as leaders because they are proven and trusted as servants." - Robert Greenleaf

23 Indisputable Qualities of Effective Leader

Visionary – Only those who can see the invisible can do the impossible.

Character – Be like a piece of rock-unyielding.

Integrity – The anchor of honor.

Courage – One person with a brave heart is a majority.

Self-Discipline – The first person to lead is you.

Initiative – With or without a follower, carry on.

Competent – If you create it, they will patronize it.

Responsible – If you cannot carry the ball, you cannot lead the team.

Passionate – Live this life and love it.

Committed – It separates a doer from a dreamer.

Determined – It is the courage of going an extra mile without being weary.

Focus – If you chase two rabbits at the same time, both will escape.

Decisiveness – This is where your destiny is shaped.

Action Oriented – A word without action is like a gun without a bullet.

Positive Attitude – If you believe you can, you will.

Possibility Thinker – three and three is equal to: six (6), nine (9) or thirty-three (33)

Discernment – Finite mind cannot solve the infinite mind. Accept things as it is.

Teachable – To keep leading, keep learning. Today a reader, tomorrow a leader.

Listener – To connect with their hearts, use your ears.

Charisma – The personal magnet attracting others to follow you.

Relational – If you get along, they will go along.

Generous – Your candle loses nothing when it lights another.

Servant – The best way to find your own self is to serve others.

"I constantly ask the question, 'How can I add value to people lives?' through this thought process, I become a leader." - Anthony Robbins

"A leader is best when people barely know he exists, not so good when people obey and acclaim him, worse when they despise him... but of a good leader who talks little when his work is done, his aim fulfilled, they will say, 'We did it ourselves'." - Lao Tzu

"As we look ahead into next century, leaders will be those who empower others... empowering leadership means bringing out the energy and capabilities that people have, and getting them to work together in a way they wouldn't do otherwise. That requires that they see the positive impact they can have and sense the opportunities. It's really up to the leader to pull the group together, get the best talent out of that group, get the group thinking about the greatest possibilities, and think how each person can contribute as a leader." - Bill Gates

"The heart that has reached utter self-forgetfulness in its love for others has not only become possessed of the highest happiness, but has entered into immortality, for it has realized the Divine." - James Allen

"I slept and dreamed that life was joy. I woke and saw that life was service. I acted, and behold, service was joy." - Rabindranath Tagore

Chapter VII

Focal
point

📖 What Matters Most

One of the prestigious manufacturing plants here in the Philippines encountered a serious technical problem, which resulted to a dramatic loss to the company's bottom line. Management decided to hire Felix Gomez, and after a few days of inspecting hundreds of gauges and dials in the control room, Felix pulled out his black marker, placed a B on one of the gauges that needed to be replaced, and sent a billing invoice for his service amounting to ₱500,000. The plant manager was surprised, the amount appearing to be excessive for just standing around a few days and putting a B mark on the apparatus that needed to be replaced. A few days later, the plant manager received a new invoice from Felix which read: "For placing B on the gauge, ₱50; for determining which gauge to place B on, ₱499,950."

This story shows an important principle in attaining success and happiness in life. Knowing where to put the B in each part of your life is the critical determinant of everything you accomplish. This B is your focal point—your Blue Chip.

"Concentrate all your thoughts on the task at hand. The sun's rays do not burn until brought to a focus."

- Alexander Graham Bell

Timeline

Birth				Growth				Death
0	10	20	30	**40**	50	60	70	**80**

In human life, three stages is constant: *Birth*, the beginning of life; *Growth*, the development and maturity of human potential; and *Death*, the entropy and decay.

Based on a study, life expectancy in modern times averages at 75 years or 27,375 days only. How do you value your days? Do you perpetually examine your present life? Are you contented with it? How do you perceive your life 20 to 30 years from now?

You are fortunate if you are just 21 years old right now for you still have 19,710 days to fulfill your life goals. But what if you are already 65 years old and your timeline left is only 3,650 days? At this point, have you already found the meaning of your life? If not, why?

Our life here on earth is temporary. We have to make the most of it while we are still here for sooner or later we will perish. The good news about life is that God gave you the freedom to choose the course of your actions—you have the independent will. God has made you responsible in every decisions you make, right or wrong. He has also endowed you with self-awareness and conscience that animal beings do not possess. You can become the architect (the creative force) of your own life. You have the ability to foresee the possible outcome of your actions. Conscience guides your inner awareness of what is right or wrong. It is the repository of timeless truths and principle that governs your behavior. You can exercise your independent will to express your self-awareness based on conscience.

True riches in life embodies not only the tangible things (material or financial wealth) but also these important intangible things—relationship, empathy, peace of mind, health, freedom, happiness, and service.

Your time is ticking away. Start to move ahead and find your purpose in life before it's too late.

Life is short, make it worthwhile!

"The purpose of our lives is to add value to the people of this generation and those that follow." - *Buckminster Fuller*

"We must never cease from exploring because at the end of all our exploration, we come back to the place where we started and we see it all for the first time." - T.S. Eliot

Dharma of Life

Who I am?

Why I am here?

What is my purpose?

What is the meaning of my life?

How can I serve?

If I have only one month to live, how will I spend my life?

These are the acid questions you should ask yourself before proceeding in the business of life. You have only but one life—a very short life and not knowing its meaning is a great loss. Not knowing your purpose in life is like a ship without a rudder—no direction, no hope. It is like chasing the wind. Knowing your purpose gives meaning to your life. It simplifies your life, motivates your soul and focuses your concerns on what matter most to you. You and only you can unfold your true identity and destiny if you know your dharma.

Dharma, a Sanskrit word, which came from the root word *dhar*, which means "to support, uphold, and nourish." It is the cosmic foundation that supports life, the sustaining force of the world, and the divine coherence of the universe. Dharma is the understanding of appropriate action in accordance with one's duty, purpose and meaning. It is the wisdom behind all things.

Can you tell me the dharma of a pen? To write, isn't it? If the pen is not used for writing, does it serve its purpose? The same is true with a candle—its main purpose is to provide light and heat. If not, a candle would be useless. In reality, this principle is the foundation in knowing the purpose and meaning of a man's life. You are not an accident. You are nature's greatest miracle and you are created for a grand purpose. Knowing and performing your dharma gives you the ability to express your true nature in unleashing the human potential—the fire within you—to achieve your life objectives and meaning. By discovering your dharma, you can develop an enormous level of integrity and influence that can shape your character and self-being.

Philosophically speaking, man's dharma is all about growth in human consciousness. Abundance is your natural state and with it comes your wealth consciousness and growth in the 4 Leverage of Life and their basic needs:

    I.   Physical/Economic Leverage - To live
        (survival and financial health)
    II. Mental/Psychological Leverage - To learn
        (growth and development)
    III. Social/Emotional Leverage - To Love
        (relationship, empathy and service)
    IV. Spiritual Leverage - To leave a legacy
        (meaning and contribution)

Balance in the 4 Leverage of Life is the key in developing and fulfilling your life worth in human standards. This is the foundation of an effective life.

Spiritually speaking, man is a trichotomous being composed of Body, Soul, and Spirit. His dharma is all about worship and service above self in God's consciousness. It all starts with God–the *true north* compass of life. It is the fulfillment of God's greatest commandment given to His unique creature–human being. To *"Love the Lord your God with all your heart, with all your soul, with all your mind, and with all your strength; and to love your neighbor as you love yourself. There is no other commandment more important than these two."*

The bedrock principle of all things that matter most in life is *love*—the sincerity of your love towards God and others. This is the highest dharma in human life, the golden rule of our spiritual maturity and the yardstick of our eternal life worth. In the end, you will realize that the natural laws of life are the law of love which is the foundation of an enlightened life.

"Life is a mission and not a career, and the purpose of all our education and knowledge is so that we can better represent HIM and serve that mission of life in HIS name and toward HIS purposes." - Stephen Richards

"The best use of life is love. The point of life is learning to love—God and people. Life minus love equals zero."
- Rick Warren

"I Am the vine; you are the branches. If you remain in Me and I in you, you will bear much fruit; apart from Me you can do nothing." - John 15:5
(Adapted from www.GodFirst.info)

The Voices Within

The *8th Habit* author Dr. Stephen Covey articulated that man in his practical sense embodies a 4 dimensional part—Body, Mind, Heart, and Spirit—or the whole person. There is a deep, built-in, almost inexpressible desire within us wanting to find our voice in life. Each dimension has an inner voice wanting to express and develop into a whole.

The following are the voices within of a whole person: for the Body, Pay me fairly; for the Mind, Use me creatively; for the Heart, Treat me kindly; and for the Spirit, Find me a meaning in serving human needs based on principles. The synergy of knowing and expressing your voices within gives you the fundamental principle and motivation in discovering your inner self and life value. It will ignite your passion to meet the needs of others with your unique talent and natural strengths in response to your conscience.

The voice of a human being is full of hope, wisdom, courage, and unlimited in its potential to serve others above self for the common good of humanity. In finding your own voice, it gives you the compelling reason in inspiring others to find also their voices in serving other human needs. This is your calling, your unique significance—your primary personal leverage.

"One man cannot do right in one department of life while he is occupied in doing wrong in any other department. Life is one indivisible whole." - Mahatma Gandhi

"I found one Law, the Law of Love; one Life, the life of adjustment to that Law; one Truth, the Truth of conquered mind and obedient heart." - James Allen

The Accounting of Life

In Chapter II of this book, you have learned the Accounting Equation:

ASSETS = LIABILITIES + CAPITAL
and
ASSETS – LIABILITIES = NET WORTH
in simple term,
NET WORTH = CAPITAL

This principle implies that the other side of the equation should always be equal to that other side of the equation to make it become a reliable and useful tool in making economic decisions.

On the same metaphor, there is an equation in the business of life that can gauge your true value as a person, which I call the life equation.

These equations tell us our true value as a person if we are in balance or not with the law of nature.

Therefore,

$$LIFE = SIN + LOVE$$
and
$$LIFE - SIN = LIFE\ WORTH$$
in simple term,
$$LIFE\ WORTH = LOVE$$

The level of love in your heart towards God and your neighbors will determine your total life worth. Are you in balance with the natural law of life?

I sought my God and my God I could not find.
I sought my soul and my soul eluded me.
I sought my brother to serve him in his need,
and I found all three—my God, my soul,
and thee.

- Anonymous

The True Person

King Solomon, the son of the great King David, was known for his divine wisdom and considered the richest man in the world during his time. When he reigned as king of Israel, he was blessed with pompous piles of fine gold, possession of vast lands and properties as far as his eyes can see; cultivated beautiful gardens and fields, raised a good breed of farm animals, carried out noteworthy philanthropic causes and aspired for greater intellectual heights than any other man.

For those hearts wanting to experience the wealth of life, King Solomon wisely advice, *"The respect for the Lord is the beginning of wisdom and true riches."* Strive by heart to become a true person;

it is a universal law that only a true one will ultimately find and reap the true riches of an abundant life.

A true person, according to King Solomon, *"Lives by the infallible laws of divine authority instead of the fallible mandates of society. He acknowledged the existence of God, who has dominion over everything that exists throughout the vast cosmic expanse. He acknowledged that money is a sacred trust from God to be employed wisely and not wasted. He envision money with awe and respect, realizing that it can be the cruelest of masters or the most excellent of slaves. He follows the wisdom of the sacred writings to guide him in the business of life. He makes the most of his earthly sojourn by living a balanced existence. He exercises love and respect for both God and man, as well as the creatures that inhabit the earth and seas, and the growing things that bestow lavish beauty or spring forth with their fruits."*

If you strive to become a true person, opportunity and financial access await you wherever you go. You will be blessed because of your personal attributes. Who you are does not matter, rather what you are from within is most important. You will never achieve 'true success' unless you possess good character and virtue, for they are the hallmark of greatness. Great character is the reward for persevering in times of difficulties and virtue is its offspring. Your primary objective is to build your character—the only thing you can take with you to eternity. Your character will serve as the seal of approval when you deal with other people.

"If you focus on principles, you empower everyone who understands those principles to act without constant monitoring, evaluating, correcting, or controlling."

- Stephen Covey

True Person's Creed

"I established for myself the following creed, which I strive to keep as a True Person. This creed reflects a befitting attitude toward money, which you should accept, commit to memory, and consciously apply. Then, day by day and little by little, the creed shall permeate your whole being and become a dynamic force of nature." - Solomon

I.   I will earn money and be fruitful, to labor six days and rest the seventh; to multiply money like a grain of corn when planted in a fertile soil; and to gain dominion over money's powerful essence that my riches may used for worthy purposes.

II. I will refrain from the love of money, for such passion causes all sorts of wickedness to manifest from the heart consequently attracting weighty troubles.

III. I will respect and follow the higher laws of the divine order, which brings about the fulfillment of my worthy aspirations by making my efforts fruitful and by giving me freedom and dominion concerning money matters.

IV. I will walk along the counsel of wise men who possess a special gift for managing money and experience bountiful harvests.

V.   I will not pursue ill-gotten monetary gains, for such profits bear an inescapable curse that is thousand folds greater than the misery of living in poverty.

VI. I will enact every monetary transaction with honesty and integrity so my heart may remain pure and my mind sober, that I may lie down in peace and sleep in safety.

VII. I will refrain from the passion for wine, pleasure, and luxury, for they are not conducive to make my fortune to grow.

VIII.   I will always measure the value of my fellowmen with far greater importance than the temporal value of my riches.

IX.   I will respect the laws of the land, under God, on the corporeal matters of life.

X.   I will let a humble spirit be my hallmark, rejecting the temptation to be dominated by pride and haughtiness because of my affluence.

XI.   I will be generous in all ways, choosing not to hoard riches that would be detrimental and grievous evil towards humanity.

XII.   I acknowledge that Almighty God owns everything that exists, including all the wealth of the world, therefore, assumes the responsibility that ownership invokes; consequently, my primary aim is to be God's spiritual possession, for all of the other details of life shall then be orderly and blessed.

"Ask the Lord to bless your plans, and you will be successful in carrying them out." - Proverbs

📖 The Fountain of Wealth

 One day during ancient times, a young man went to a spiritual master seeking for the key to abundance, to which the master replied, "There are two goddesses who reside in the heart of a human being, and although you love both goddesses, you must pay more attention to one of them." "One of the goddesses is *Wisdom* - pursue her, love her, and give her all your attention. When you pay more attention to wisdom, the other goddess, *Wealth*, will become extremely jealous and seek your attention. She will follow you wherever you go and the wealth you desire will be yours forever."

"Principles represent the deeper well. This deeper well of principles supplies all the shallower wells and root structures of empowerment, quality, producing more for less, sustainability, scalability and agility." - Stephen Covey

The Gospel of Wealth

King Solomon said, *"In order to achieve financial freedom by following God's financial guidelines, you must make certain destiny-changing commitments:*

"Commit yourself to honor the Lord with your life, which will give your existence profound meaning and purpose. Spiritual enlightenment contributes to good character, which is the cornerstone of true riches. No amount of wealth can set you free to live your fullest and atone for poverty of character. Only through meaningful relationship with your Maker can you accomplish these things.

"Commit yourself to honor the Lord with your wealth, for your Creator is the eternal proprietor of everything that exist, property and wealth included. The best way for you to honor the most high is with your wealth, for your heartstring is attached securely to your purse string. The Almighty will test the sincerity of your heart with the challenge of sharing your finances with others who are in need. Nothing reveals your true character as much as the uses to which you put your money.

"Commit yourself to honor the Lord by discovering why your Maker supplies you with more money than is required to meet your own financial needs. You have more so that you may give more, and you will receive more, that you may then give again. Joyfully give a generous portion of all you earn and find much favor with the Great Provider."

If you want your life to have a significant impact, focus and commit it with intense passion towards His purposes.

"Gold finds its way into the purse of a man who gives more and better service, as surely as the sun rises in the east." - Solomon

"It is through blessed abundance that we can enjoy the true value of life." - Rane A. Panaligan

📖 The Bamboo

 In a field near the river, there was a cluster of tall bamboos, and one day, the farmer stood before the tallest one and said, "My dear friend, I need you." "Sir," said the bamboo, "use me in any way you want; I am ready." Then the farmer's voice became a bit serious and he said, "In order to use you, I've got to split you in half, cut off all your branches and leaves, and causing you more pain, take away even your heart and your insides." The majestic bamboo, smitten to the core, allowed the farmer to cut and prune him as he wished, and after the farmer cut down the bamboo, lopped off its branches and leaves, split it down the middle, and then hollowed out its insides, the farmer connected the bamboo with the spring, and let it carry the water to the fields to make them fruitful, a source of great blessing to the people.

And so it was that when the bamboo had been cut down, dismembered and split right down the middle, it became a source of great blessing to the people.

"This is the true joy in life, that being used for a purpose recognized by yourself as a mighty one. I am of the opinion that my life belongs to the whole community and as long as I live it is my privilege to do for it whatever I

can. Life is no 'brief candle' to me. It is a sort of splendid torch which I have got to hold up for the moment and I want it burn as brightly as possible before handing it on to future generations." - George Bernard Shaw

📖 The Carpenter

An elderly carpenter told his contractor-employer of his plans to retire to enjoy life with his family. The contractor felt sad and asked his dutiful worker to build one more house before he goes. The carpenter said yes but his heart was not in his work so he built a lousy house and when he finished his work, his employer handed him the front-door key to it, and said, "This is your house." The carpenter felt ashamed, thinking if only he had known he was building his own house, he would have done it all so differently.

Thus, it all depends on us. We build our lives a day at a time, often using less of our best efforts. Suddenly we realize that we have to live the life we have faintly built. If we could live our life all over again, we would do it much differently. However, we cannot go back.

You are the carpenter of your own life and each day you hammer a nail or erect a wall of life. Someone said, "Life is a do-it-yourself project." The attitude and the choices you make today will build the "house" you will dwell in tomorrow. Build it wisely!

"And in the end it's not the years in your life that count. It's the life in your years." - Abraham Lincoln

📖 Acres of Diamond

A wealthy Persian by the name of Al Haphid enticed by the discovery of diamonds in Europe, sold his farm and travelled to look for the diamond mines but found none. He spent all his money and became very poor and in deep desperation, he drowned himself in the river. Meanwhile, the man who bought the farm of the Persian man had found the diamonds sparkling in the sand near the garden brook. And that's how the great diamond mines of Galconda–the most magnificent diamond mine in all the history of the world was discovered.

My friend, you do not need to look beyond or go farther in a strange land to find your dream fortune. It is here already!

The hidden wealth machine you have been searching for is right here in the entrepreneurial business and network marketing business that you might not have noticed or considered yet in your wealth-building plan.

Learn the system with an open mind and grow with it. This might be the acres of diamond you have been looking for quite a long time. Start digging now before somebody else takes your place.

Seek and you shall find!

"Enduring wealth comes to no man until he prepares himself to receive it." - Solomon

"Where the determination is, the way can be found."
– Arkad

📖 Life is What We Make It

 A wise old man living in Himalayas occasionally treks down into the local village to entertain the people with his special abilities, one of which is to tell what object is in a container or what does a person thinks. A few boys planned to ridicule him and one of them caught a bird and enclosed it in his grip. The boy knew that the wise man would know what would be in his hands so he asked if the bird is dead or alive. The old man looked straight in the boy's eyes and said calmly, "My child,

the life of that bird which you now hold is already in your hands as you choose it, and so it is also with your life."

Dear friend, the fulfillment or non-fulfillment of your dreams and aspirations in life is in your hands right now. The choice is yours.

Today is the start of the rest of your life

"If you do nothing, nothing will happen. If you do something, something will happen. The worst that can happen is that you might finish with nothing, which is what you started with. Therefore, there is really nothing to lose. There is however, a wonderful opportunity to have a rich and fulfilling life." - Stuart Moore

Focal Thoughts

Thought Is the original source of all wealth, all success, all material gain, all discoveries and inventions, and of all achievement.

— Claude Bristol

ATTITUDE

The winner's edge is not in a gifted birth, a high IQ, or in talent. The winner's edge is all in the attitude, not aptitude. Attitude is the criterion for success.

— Denis Waitley

You cannot control what happens to you, but you can control your attitude toward what happens to you, and in that, you will be mastering change rather than allowing it to master you.

— Brian Tracy

Whether we regard difficulties in life as misfortunes or whether we view them as good fortune depends entirely on how much we have forged our inner determination. It all depends on our attitude or inner state of life.

— Daisaku Ikeda

BELIEF

A man can be as great as he wants to be. If you believe in yourself and have the courage, the determination, the dedication, the competitive drive and if you are willing to sacrifice the little things in life and pay the price for the things that are worthwhile, it can be done.

— Vince Lombardi

When you develop yourself to the point where your belief in yourself is so strong that you know you can accomplish anything you put your mind to, your future will be unlimited.

– Brian Tracy

If you develop the absolute sense of certainty that powerful beliefs provide, then you can get yourself to accomplish virtually anything, Including those things that other people are certain are impossible.

– Anthony Robbins

COMMITMENT
The quality of a person's life is in direct proportion to their commitment to excellence, regardless of their chosen field of endeavor.

– Vince Lombardi

Do all the good you can, by all the means you can, in all the ways you can, in all the places you can, at all the times you can, to all the people you can, as long as ever you can.

– John Wesley

I believe life is constantly testing us for our level of commitment, and life's greatest rewards are reserved for those who demonstrate a never-ending commitment to act until they achieve.

– Anthony Robbins

COURAGE
Courage is the force that makes our lives brilliant. True courage and adventure is found in exploring the meaning of life and discovering the reason for your existence. Even greater joy and fulfillment is found in the persistent struggle to contribute to others' happiness.

– Daisaku Ikeda

You will never do anything in this world without courage. It is the greatest quality of the mind next to honor.

— Aristotle

Courage is going from failure to failure without losing enthusiasm.

—Winston Churchill

CHANGE

Some men see things as they are and say, "Why?" I dream of things that never were and say, "Why not?"

— George Bernard Shaw

Change will not come if we wait for some other person or some other time. We are the ones we've been waiting for. We are the change that we seek.

— Barack Obama

The truth is that our finest moments are most likely to occur when we are feeling deeply uncomfortable, unhappy, or unfulfilled. For it is only in such moments, propelled by our discomfort, that we are likely to step out of our ruts and start searching for different ways or truer answers.

— M. Scott Peck

EXCELLENCE

Our work should be our *obra maestra* or masterpiece where we pour out all that we've got to insure success and excellence.

— Jose Pardo

You must never be satisfied; you must always try to be better than your previous self.

— Evelyn Singson

Live your life as though your every act were to become a universal law.

– Immanuel Kant

FOCUS

A man of sense is never discouraged by difficulties; he redoubles his industry and his diligence, he perseveres and infallibly prevails at last.

– Lord Chesterfield

Most people have no idea of the giant capacity we can immediately command when we focus all of our resources on mastering a single area of our lives.

– Anthony Robbins

Present-moment living, getting in touch with your now, is at the heart of effective living. When you think about it, there really is no other moment you can live. Now is all there is, and the future is just another present moment to live when it arrives.

– Wayne Dyer

GOAL

Your goal must be clear, written, and specific. They must be believable and achievable. They must be accompanied by written plans and schedules for their accomplishment. You must work on them every day.

– Brian Tracy

There is one quality which one must possess to win, and that is definiteness of purpose, the knowledge of what one wants, and a burning desire to possess it.

– Napoleon Hill

It is those who concentrate on but one thing at a time who advance in this world.

– Og Mandino

PASSION

The most powerful weapon on earth is the human soul on fire.

– Ferdinand Foch

One's true worth as a human being is not a matter of outward appearance or title but derives from the breadth of one's spirit. Everything comes down to faith and conviction. It is what is in one's heart and the substance of one's actions that count.

– Daisaku Ikeda

If there is no passion in your life, then have you really lived? Find your passion, whatever it may be. Become it, and let it become you and you will find great things happen for you.

– T. Alan Armstrong

POSSIBILITY

There are no limits to what you can accomplish if you develop absolute clarity about who you are and what you want and then throw your whole heart into doing your job better than anyone else. This commitment will lead to unlimited opportunities.

– Brian Tracy

All positive change in the world comes from our ideas of what we believe is possible.

– Alexandra Jamieson

Only those who will risk going too far can possibly find out how far one can go.

– T.S. Eliot

POTENTIAL

Each person possesses a precious inner treasure of infinite worth. To remain unaware of this and stumble about in spiritual poverty is a tragic waste. In contrast, a person fully awakened to the jewel-like dignity of their own life is capable of truly respecting that treasure in others.

– Daisaku Ikeda

Whatever your discipline, become a student of excellence in all things. Take every opportunity to observe people who manifest the qualities of mastery. These models of excellence will inspire you and guide you toward the fulfillment of your highest potential.

– Tony Buzan

Anything that has been accomplished by any other human being in the physical realm is within the field of possibility.

– Wayne Dyer

PURPOSE

The purpose of human life is to serve: to show compassion and the will to help others.

–Albert Schweitzer

No man or woman is an island. To exist just for yourself is meaningless. You can achieve the most satisfaction when you feel related to some greater purpose in life, something greater than yourself.

– Dennis Waitley

Strange is our situation here upon earth. Each of us comes for a short visit, not knowing why, yet sometimes seeming to divine a purpose. From the standpoint of daily life, however, there is one thing we do know: that man is here for the sake of other men.

– Albert Einstein

SELF MASTERY
The first and best victory is to conquer self.

– Plato

The absolute truth is that the 'I' is perfect and complete; the real 'I' is spiritual and can therefore never be less than perfect; it can never have any lack, limitation, or disease.

– Charles Haanel

People do not grow when their environment is too comfortable, when they are not challenged. It is in the midst of suffering and hardship that strength of character is formed.

– Daisaku Ikeda

SERVICE
How can I be useful, of what service can I be? There is something inside me, what can it be?

– Vincent Van Gogh

Whoever renders service to many puts himself in line for greatness - great wealth, great return, great satisfaction, great reputation, and great joy.

– Jim Rohn

I don't know what your destiny will be, but one thing I do know: the only ones among you who will be really happy are those who have sought and found how to serve.

– Albert Schweitzer

TEAM BUILDING
Teamwork is the ability to work together toward a common vision. The ability to direct individual accomplishments toward

organizational objectives. It is the fuel that allows common people to attain uncommon results.

– Andrew Carnegie

The leaders who work most effectively, it seems to me, never say 'I'. And that's not because they have trained themselves not to say 'I'. They don't think 'I'. They think 'we'; they think 'team'. They understand their job to be to make the team function. They accept responsibility and don't sidestep it, but 'we' gets the credit. This is what creates trust, what enables you to get the task done.

– Peter Drucker

What we need to do is learn to work in the system, by which I mean that everybody, every team, every platform, every division, every component is there not for individual competitive profit or recognition, but for contribution to the system as a whole on a win-win basis.

– Edward Deming

VALUES
The ultimate value of life depends upon awareness and the power of contemplation rather than upon mere survival.

– Aristotle

The value of a man should be seen in what he gives and not in what he is able to receive.

– Albert Einstein

You live from the inside out. The core of your being is composed of your deepest beliefs about what is right and good in human condition. Your values determine your emotions, your motivations, and your responses to the world around you.

– Brian Tracy

Bibliography

The ideas and concepts in this book have either been adapted or inspired by the following books, which are highly recommended for reading:

American Bible Society. *Good News Bible 2nd Edition*. 1992.

The Zondervan Corp. *The Devotional Study Bible (New International Version*. Manila. Philippine Bible Society).

Warren, Rick. *The Purpose Driven Life – What On Earth Am I Here For*. Manila: OMF Literature Inc., 2002.

Counsel, John. *The Beginner's Guide to Multi-Level Marketing*. Kuala Lumpur, Malaysia: Synergy Books International.

De Garmo, Scott and Tartaglia, Louis A. M.D. *Heart to Heart – The Real Power of Network Marketing*. Rocklin, CA: Prima Publishing, 1999.

Kalench, John. *Being the Best You Can Be in MLM*. U.S.A.

Schreiter, Tom. *Big Al Tells All—The Recruiting System (Sponsoring Magic)*. U.S.A. KAAS Publishing, 1985.

Tai Chai Lessons For Success in MLM Book 1, Eddy Chai, Copyright 2002

Copycat Marketing 101, How to Copycat Your Way To Wealth by Burke Hedges, Copyright 2009

Pease, Allan. *Questions are the Answers: How to get to 'Yes' in Network Marketing.* Australia: Pease International Pty Ltd., 2000.

Go, Josiah. *Build, Grow and Sustain Your Network Marketing Distribution Business.* Quezon City, Phils.: Design Plus, 2000.

Lim, Billi P.S. *Dare to Fail – From KSE (Kia-Su Economy) to KBE (Knowledge-Based Economy).* Malaysia: Hardknocks Factory SDN. BHD, 2000.

Hansen, Mark Victor & Allen, Robert G. *The One Minute Millionaire.* New York: Harmony Books, 2002.

Waschka, Larry. *Getting Rich (The complete Idiots Guide).* Macmillan Publishing, 1999.

Anthony, Robert N., Reece, James S. and Hertenstein, Julie H. *Accounting: Text and Cases.* 9th Ed. U.S.A:Irwin Publishing,1994.

Heineche, William E. with Marsh, Jonathan. *The Entrepreneur: 21 Golden Rules for the Global Business Manager.* Singapore: John Wiley and Sons, Inc., 2000.

Tracy, Brian. *Focal Point.* New York: Mc Graw-Hill. 2002.

Tracy, Brian. *The 21 Success Secrets of Self- Made Millionaires.* Asia: Mc Graw-Hill Education, 2001.

Peterson, Erlend CFP. *Money Changes Everything—Seven Simple Steps That Will Make Money Work For You.* New Delhi, India: Anmol Publications Pvt. Ltd., 2002.

Orcullo, N.A. Jr, Ph. D. *Contemporary Entrepreneurs.* Mandaluyong City, Phils: Academic Publishing Corp., 2000.

Bland, Glenn. *Legends of the Golden Scrolls: Ageless Secrets for Building Wealth.* Malaysia: Synergy Books International, 1996.

Hunter, James C. *The Servant: A Simple Story about the True Essence of Leadership.* U.S.A.: Prima Publishing, 1998.

Covey, Stephen R. *The 7 Habits of Highly Effective People.* New York: Simon and Schuster, Inc., 1989.

Covey, Stephen R. *The 8th Habit: From Effectiveness to Greatness.* New York.: Simon and Schuster, Inc., 2004.

Covey, Stephen R. *Principle-Centered Leadership.* New York: Simon and Schuster, Inc., 1991

Chopra, Deepak. *The Seven Spiritual Laws of Success. California,* U.S.A.: New World Library and Amber-Allen Publishing, 1996.

Chopra, Deepak. *Creating Affluence: A to Z Steps to a Richer Life.* California, U.S.A.: Thomas Nelson, Inc., 1998.

Colayco, Fransisco J. *Wealth Within Your Reach – Pera Mo, Palaguin Mo.* Philis: Colayco Foundation for Education, Inc., 2004.

Maxwell, John C. *The 21 Irrefutable Laws of Leadership.* U.S.A.: Thomas Nelson, Inc., 1998.

Maxwell, John C. *Developing the Leader Within You.* U.S.A.: Thomas Nelson, Inc., 1993.

Maxwell, John C. *Failing Forward- Turning Mistakes Into Stepping Stones For Success*. U.S.A.: Thomas Nelson, Inc., 2000.

Hunter, James C. *The World's Most Powerful Leadership Principle: How to Become a Servant Leader*. New York: Crown Business Publishing, 2004.

Hou, Wee Chow; Sheang, Lee Kai; and Hidajat Bambang Walujo. *Sun Tzu: War and Management*. Singapore: Addison – Wesley Publishing Co. Inc., 1991.

Senn-Delaney Leadership Consulting Group. *Leadership, Teambuilding, & Culture Change—A Guide to Organizational & Personal Effectiveness*. New York: The Leadership Press Inc., 1994.

Bach, Richard. *Jonathan Livingston Seagull: A Story*. New York: Macmillan Publishing Co., Inc., 1999.

Clason, George S. *The Richest Man in Babylon*. New York: New American Library, Penguin Putnam Inc., 1988.

Mandino, Og. *The Greatest Secret in the World*. New York: Federick Fell Publishers, Inc., 1978.

Hill, Napoleon. *Think & Grow Rich*. U.S.A.: The Random House Publishing Group, 1960.

Kiyosaki, Robert T. with Lechter, Sharon L. *Rich Dad, Poor Dad*. New York: Warner Books, Inc. 1998

Kiyosaki, Robert T. with Lechter, Sharon L. *Cash Flow Quadrant*. New York: Warner Books, Inc. 1998, 1999.

Kiyosaki, Robert T. with Lechter, Sharon L. *Retire Young, Retire Rich*. New York: Warner Books, Inc. 2002.

Eker, T. Harv. *Secrets of the Millionnaire Mind*. New York: Harper Collins Publishers Inc. and Piatkus Books Ltd. 2005.

Allen, James. *The Secret of Success*. New Delhi: New Dawn Press, Inc. 2004

Adams, Brian. *How To Succeed - Dynamic Mind Principles That Transform Your Life*. Horwitz Publications, 1969.

Mihalic, Frank SVD. *1000 Stories You Can Use, Volume One*. Manila: Logos Publication, 1987, 15th Printing 2002.

Conwell, Russell. *Acres of Diamond*: New York.

Khera Shiv. *You Can Win*. India: New Dawn Press Group. Revised Edition, 2002.

www.ingramcontent.com/pod-product-compliance
Lightning Source LLC
Chambersburg PA
CBHW031054180526
45163CB00002BA/834

* 9 7 8 1 4 9 0 7 3 8 5 1 2 *